Gary Mehigan's
Comfort Food

Gary Mehigan's Comfort food

Food photography by
Dean Cambray

LANTERN
an imprint of
PENGUIN BOOKS

Contents

To Frederick Sharman, my grandfather,

who was an inspiration to one little boy,

and to my darling wife, Mandy, and beautiful daughter, Jenna —

I couldn't do all of this without you.

Introduction

A lot of water has passed under the bridge since I first stepped into the kitchens at The Connaught Hotel London in 1986. I was a fresh-faced eighteen year-old with a Hotel and Catering Diploma tucked under my arm. My friends thought I was mad – cooking was seen as something subservient, so when was I going to get a proper job?

I encountered a world that was hierarchical and steeped in tradition – you knew your place and twelve-hour days were the norm: it inspired me. I will never forget that first day; it felt chaotic and electric and the concentration required was intense, what with chefs running here and there, huge boilers full of celeriac, artichokes, stocks and sauces, and steamers and stovetops that bellowed out a brutal heat. I had never seen food like it, there was the best of everything, including brown crabs, lobsters, langoustines, turbot, brill, whole Welsh lamb, sides of dry-aged Scottish beef, grouse, snipe, woodcock and wild ducks. In the larder, chefs were peeling kilos of Perigord truffles over a large white tablecloth to catch all the peelings. The earthy, heady smell filled the kitchen – it was mesmerising. I was in heaven.

Twenty years on and this industry has seen me travel around the world, it has channelled my creativity and fuelled my love for food, but most of all it has taught me to embrace the moment – people, places, textures, flavours and sensations that I am sure only a cook can know.

I love to cook at home and in my restaurants – I love the touch, feeling and process of putting gorgeous food onto a plate. It keeps me peeling, roasting, frying, poaching and baking with the best of them – I love it! In fact, I look forward to the day that I'm sixty-five – not to retire, I won't. What I will do is have chickens in my garden, grow my own vegetables and make my own (undoubtedly contraband) beverages from my apples and plums. My Grandad, bless his soul, would certainly approve!

It was my grandfather that inspired my career choice. He was the world to me when I was a little boy growing up on Hayling Island off the South Coast of England. He was a well-regarded chef but that meant nothing to me at the time. In his retirement he nurtured a beautiful English garden. I remember the big, ugly cooking apples and prickly greengages that were so sour they made you wince, but tasted brilliant in his sugary apple pies. The veggie patch had tall lines of tangled runner beans and the greenhouse was full of tomatoes. I remember feeding worms to his giant goldfish, one of which was called 'Guzzle Guts'; it still makes me smile to this day. Mum would find out that I had eaten cabbage for dinner – finely shredded, cooked in a little butter with bacon and garlic – and wolfed down the lot. It drove her mad because, of course, when she cooked cabbage, it never tasted the same.

Thinking about the food that I want to eat is easy. I now know what I love – it has to be deeply satisfying, beg me to plunge my spoon or fork back in for more and take me somewhere I want to be – simple really.

When I was younger I thought that great food was exclusive to grand restaurants. However, some of the worst, most impersonal and improbable food can be found in flashy restaurants. Often they miss the point, which is known in the trade as 'perfect delivery – imperfect experience'. The waiter smiles but doesn't mean it, the food looks fabulous but doesn't hit the spot. As chefs we are often guilty of cooking to impress and to demonstrate our skills and creativity but we often forget the simplest of things. We need to get out of the kitchen from time to time. When we finally do it's a revelation. We discover that not everyone has traveled to our restaurant for a food epiphany. There are people engrossed in conversation, looking lovingly into each others eyes, laughing, arguing or doing business. Food is more often than not just one element of their time together; it is the conduit for so many things.

So what is the perfect meal? It's as much to do with place and company as it is about contrast in texture and flavour. I think of fish and chips by the sea, the crumply paper, the soggy chips, the squawking seagulls and crashing waves – a summer holiday in a perfect place, eating the perfect meal. It has to be made and served with love and generosity of spirit. The best cooks love to serve; they want to feed you, they can't help themselves, and they can't let you leave without knowing that you are happy and, of course, full and about to burst.

That being said, everyone has a different idea of comfort food. That's the way it should be. When I started thinking about writing this book, I decided to include the first dishes that sprang to mind, trust my instincts and provide recipes that I love to cook myself – in other words, my comfort food.

Whether I'm cooking comfort food or more top-end cheffy dishes, I like to know where my produce has come from – the less it has to travel, the fresher it will be (and it is better for the planet too).

If we take an interest in where and how our food is grown we will naturally end up doing the right thing. Don't buy cherries from California or beans from Kenya; the only reason supermarkets stock them is because we buy them. Buy foods when they are in season, local, plentiful and good value for money. We should also demand that the animals we eat have been reared humanely and responsibly. There is no place for cage chickens; it is not right and we all know it. Try adding variety to your diet by buying different cuts of meat, offal and a range of grains, pulses and vegetables.

Food brings us together. The time around the family table, whether it's the two of you or a troop of hungry mouths, is a special time – time that you can never get back. Discuss your day, the highs and lows; tell each other your thoughts and feelings.

The best advice I can give you as a cook is to enjoy all that food brings to your life. Make the very most of the recipes and celebrate the people you love and the food that you eat together.

Breakfast, Brunch and Lunch

Ricotta Pancakes with Date and Banana Butter

Ricotta pancakes have been on the breakfast menus of my restaurants since day one. While there is always a place for thin pancakes or crepes, thick pancakes are the go for a hearty and satisfying breakfast. There's nothing better than sitting down to a plate of fluffy pancakes with a latte in your hand, the gentle warmth of the morning sun and the promise of an easy hour to read the Sunday paper – ah . . . Wake up Gary, you are dreaming again, the kids are screaming and it's time to get a move on!

1   For the date and banana butter, whip the butter with hand-held electric beaters until light and creamy, then stir in the dates and banana. Set aside.

2   Sift the flour and salt together, then add the sugar. In another bowl, whisk the egg and milk together, then add to the flour mixture. Beat well with a whisk to remove any lumps.

3   Melt the butter in a frying pan over low heat until it bubbles and becomes nut-brown. Whisk the burnt butter into the batter, then stir in the ricotta; don't worry if there are a few lumps.

4   Heat a heavy-based non-stick frying pan over medium heat with a drizzle of oil or knob of butter. Place a small ladleful of the batter into the hot pan and cook for 2–3 minutes. When bubbles appear on the surface, gently turn the pancake over and cook for another 2–3 minutes. Transfer the pancake to a plate and repeat with the remaining batter. You should end up with 8 pancakes.

5   Serve the pancakes with the date and banana butter and maple syrup, or with extra sugar and lemon wedges, if using.

Serves 4

250 g self-raising flour
pinch of table salt
50 g caster sugar
1 free-range egg
300 ml milk
25 g unsalted butter
75 g firm ricotta, drained
    and crumbled
vegetable oil or extra butter,
    for cooking
maple syrup or caster sugar
    and lemon wedges
    (optional), to serve

DATE AND BANANA BUTTER
125 g unsalted butter,
    chopped, softened
75 g fresh dates such as medjool,
    pitted and chopped
2 small bananas, mashed

Notes

- *The addition of burnt butter to the batter adds extra flavour and improves the texture of the pancakes; however, it can be omitted.*

- *I like to add a little ricotta to my pancakes. Not only does it create an interesting texture, but it adds a little bulk to the dish and it is also good for you.*

Mushroom Bruschetta with Soft-poached Eggs

Serves 4

60 ml olive oil
2 large cloves garlic, thinly sliced
4 slices dense sourdough bread
table salt
60 ml white-wine vinegar
4 free-range eggs
freshly ground white pepper
300 g mixed exotic mushrooms,
    such as enoki, oyster and
    wood ear, trimmed
2 large portabello or
    king brown mushrooms,
    trimmed, thickly sliced
25 g unsalted butter
2 tablespoons shredded
    flat-leaf parsley

Notes

- For perfect poached eggs, start with super-fresh eggs as this means the yolks and whites will hold their shape rather than dispersing when they hit the hot water.

- Make sure you have a pan with lots of boiling water ready, as this gives the eggs space to cook evenly and ensures that the water continues to simmer during cooking.

- A good splash of white-wine or champagne vinegar helps to set the protein in the egg white, resulting in a firm, nicely-rounded poached egg.

Good bruschetta, like a good pizza base, should be the vehicle for showcasing great ingredients at their seasonal best. I start with a crusty, dense sourdough with loads of flavour. When it comes to toppings, grilled asparagus, buffalo mozzarella, good-quality ham, smoked trout or soft figs are just some of the fabulous options. In the height of summer, one of my all-time-favourites is to stand by the barbecue armed with a couple of garlic cloves, great extra virgin olive oil, sea salt flakes and cut ripe tomatoes, then squish and drizzle these onto the charred bread. Here I've chosen to use gutsy garlic-infused portabello and exotic mushrooms paired with perfectly soft-poached eggs to make a substantial brekky.

1 Heat the oil in a non-stick frying pan over medium heat. Cook the garlic for 2–3 minutes or until light-golden and crisp. Remove the garlic from the pan, then drain on paper towel. Pour the oil into a small bowl, leaving a little in the pan, then set aside.

2 Grill the bread on a chargrill pan or barbecue grill-plate over high heat and keep warm.

3 Bring a saucepan of water to the boil over high heat, then add a pinch of salt and the vinegar. Make sure that the water is gently turning over (boiling) at a simmer. Working quickly, crack one egg at a time into the simmering water, leaving a little space between each egg. Poach the eggs for 3–4 minutes. Gently lift the eggs from the water with a slotted spoon, then drain on paper towel and season with a pinch of salt and pepper.

4 Meanwhile, heat the non-stick frying pan over high heat. Add the mushrooms and fry for 4 minutes or until golden, then add the butter and cook for another 1 minute. Add the parsley and remove from the heat.

5 Divide the mushrooms and eggs between the warm toast, sprinkle with the crisp garlic, then drizzle with a little of the reserved garlic-infused oil and serve.

Raspberry Muffins

This muffin recipe is a cracker. Don't ask me what the sour cream and oil are for, they just taste great. Raspberry muffins would have to be one of my absolute favourites, but you could easily substitute any fresh or dried fruit, nuts or chocolate chips (or all of these if it takes your fancy). I prefer to use two large six-hole muffin trays, so if you are using the smaller twelve-hole cupcake-sized trays it may make double the number, but don't let this deter you. You can always keep half of the batter in the fridge for several days, ready for the next time you want to whip up a batch. Alternatively, bake the lot in batches and freeze leftovers to add to the kids' lunchboxes. Not the best way to enjoy them, perhaps, but I'll forgive you – I know you are busy!

1   Preheat a fan-forced oven to 180°C.

2   Place 12 large paper cases into the lightly greased holes of two 6-hole capacity muffin trays.

3   Sift the flour, salt, bicarbonate of soda and baking powder into a bowl. Beat the eggs and sugar in the bowl of an electric mixer until pale and thickened. Beat the egg mixture on a low speed, slowly drizzling in the oil and adding the flour mixture. Mix the batter until just incorporated, then add the sour cream and mix for 1 minute to ensure all the ingredients are combined.

4   Gently stir in the raspberries. Spoon the batter into the prepared muffin tray holes to just below the tops of the paper cases. Bake for 15 minutes, then remove from the oven and leave to cool in the pan. Serve warm or at room temperature, dusted with icing sugar, if desired.

Makes 12

360 g plain flour
pinch of table salt
1 teaspoon bicarbonate of soda
2 teaspoons baking powder
4 free-range eggs
270 g caster sugar
180 ml vegetable oil
275 ml sour cream
250 g raspberries
icing sugar (optional), for dusting

Notes

- *As with all baking, I suggest that you follow the recipe and use a fan-forced oven that keeps a constant temperature.*

- *When adding fruit or other flavourings to the batter avoid over-mixing as this results in a tough texture. Fresh or frozen berries and chopped fruit such as banana or pears are perfect additions, as are dried fruit and chocolate chips.*

- *Don't over-fill the paper cases – fill them to just below the top to allow room for the muffin to rise and not overflow as it bakes.*

French Toast with Honey Cumquats

I am a sucker for a good French toast and this version qualifies – it is crisp and sweet on the outside and soft and well-soaked with egg on the inside. I'm not so keen on the bacon and maple syrup rendition that is popular, but some Honey Cumquats or a flavoured butter such as the Date and Banana Butter on page 2 (or try whipped butter with marmalade) will seal the deal. Good-quality bread is a must.

1   For the honey cumquats, bring the honey to the boil in a small saucepan over medium heat. Add the vanilla, cinnamon, star anise and cumquats and simmer for 30 minutes or until tender. Set aside.

2   Preheat a fan-forced oven to 120°C.

3   Crack the eggs into a wide bowl and add the milk, sugar and cinnamon. Soak the bread slices in the egg mixture well until saturated. Leave to stand for a few minutes.

4   Heat a little oil in a large heavy-based non-stick frying pan over medium heat for 3 minutes. Lay 4 slices of the bread in the pan and cook for 3 minutes or until golden brown, then add 15 g of the butter to the pan and allow it to bubble around the bread before turning the bread over. Cook the second side for 3 minutes or until golden brown. Lower the heat if required. Transfer the French toast to a paper towel-lined baking tray and keep warm in the oven. Repeat with the remaining oil, bread and butter.

5   Divide the French toast between 4 plates, then spoon over the warm cumquats and syrup, sprinkle with a scattering of flaked almonds, add a knob of butter and serve.

Serves 4

6 free-range eggs
200 ml milk
2 tablespoons white sugar
1 teaspoon ground cinnamon
1 round sourdough loaf, crust-ends and crusts discarded, cut into 12 thick slices
30 ml vegetable oil
30 g unsalted butter, plus extra to serve
flaked almonds, to serve

HONEY CUMQUATS
150 g honey
1 vanilla pod, split and seeds scraped
1 cinnamon stick
2 star anise
30 cumquats

Notes

- *Leave enough time for the egg mixture to soak into the bread (3–4 minutes should do it), pressing the bread into the mixture with your fingers.*

- *A good-quality sourdough makes all the difference in flavour so splash out.*

- *When making the Honey Cumquats, a little water can be added to the pan, if required. However, this will not be necessary if the cumquats are soft and juicy.*

- *Leftover Honey Cumquats will keep in a sterilised jar in the fridge for up to 4 weeks. They are also fantastic spread on thick toast for brekky or serve them with ice cream for an easy dessert.*

Green Eggs and Ham

There is an art to making a good hollandaise – or is there? It is all about understanding and controlling temperature to achieve a light, satiny, smooth sabayon (emulsified egg yolk-based sauce). You don't have to add too much butter if you'd prefer not to – I don't and as a result my version is lighter than most and makes me feel better about eating it! Despite all those calories, as a treat once in a while, you can't beat my green eggs and ham.

1   For the green hollandaise, plunge the parsley and spinach into a saucepan of boiling salted water for 2 minutes. Drain and refresh under cold running water, then squeeze dry. Puree in a food processor or blender, then set aside.

2   Melt the butter in a small saucepan over low heat and allow the whey and solids to settle, then ladle off the clear melted butter and discard the whey. (This is called clarified butter.)

3   Place the shallot, wine, vinegar, bay leaf and peppercorns in a small saucepan and reduce over high heat by two-thirds. Remove from the heat and discard the bay leaf and peppercorns. Add the yolks to the pan and whisk until foamy and light, then place the pan over low heat and continue whisking until the mixture forms a thick ribbon when you lift the whisk from the pan. Be careful not to scramble the mixture – remove from the heat if you feel it is getting away from you. Slowly whisk in the melted butter, then season with salt, pepper and the lemon. Set aside.

4   Bring a saucepan of water to the boil over high heat, then add a pinch of salt and the vinegar. Make sure that the water is gently turning over (boiling) at a simmer. Working quickly, crack one egg at a time into the simmering water, leaving a little space between each egg. Poach the eggs for 3–4 minutes. Gently lift the eggs from the water with a slotted spoon, then drain on paper towel and season with a pinch of salt and pepper.

5   Toast the bread, then spread with butter. Divide the toast between 4 plates, then top each one with a slice of ham and a poached egg. Whisk the herb puree into the hollandaise at the last minute, then spoon over the eggs. Toss the rocket with a drizzle of olive oil, then place a small handful of leaves on each plate and serve.

Serves 4

table salt
dash of champagne vinegar
8 free-range eggs
freshly ground black pepper
8 slices sourdough bread
butter, for spreading
8 slices good-quality ham
rocket and extra virgin
   olive oil, to serve

GREEN HOLLANDAISE
1 cup flat-leaf parsley leaves
1 cup baby spinach
table salt
150 g unsalted butter, chopped
2 shallots, finely chopped
375 ml white wine
250 ml champagne vinegar
1 fresh bay leaf
4 black peppercorns
3 free-range egg yolks
sea salt flakes and freshly
   ground black pepper
squeeze of lemon juice

Notes

· *For perfect poached eggs, start with super-fresh eggs as this means the yolks and whites will hold their shape rather than dispersing when they hit the hot water.*

· *Make sure you have a pan ready with lots of boiling water, as this gives the eggs lots of space to cook evenly and ensures that the water continues to simmer during cooking.*

· *A good splash of white-wine or champagne vinegar helps to set the protein in the egg white, resulting in a firm and nicely-rounded poached egg.*

Almond Granola with Watermelon and Labneh

Serves 6

180 g rolled oats
100 g mixed nuts (such as walnuts, almonds and cashews) and flaked coconut
pinch of sea salt
½ teaspoon ground cinnamon
3 tablespoons honey, plus extra to serve
1 teaspoon vanilla paste (see page 197)
60 ml almond oil
190 g mixed dried fruit, such as raisins, dates, figs, pear, apricots and cranberries
watermelon and sunflower seeds (optional), to serve

LABNEH (OPTIONAL)
250 g thick Greek-style yoghurt

While there are many different mueslis and granolas on the market (so you might feel spoilt for choice), the point is that, until you've made your own, you'll never know how easy it is. Health food stores (and even your local supermarket) now sell all sorts of things you can pop in, such as puffed rice or wheat and a huge variety of nuts and dried fruits. My recipe uses honey, however, you could always use brown sugar or maple syrup. The choice of seeds, nuts and fruits is entirely yours – it can be varied based on what you like. You might start with my recipe but before too long, it will be yours!

1   For the labneh, if making, place the yoghurt on a sheet of muslin, then wrap and suspend over a bowl in the fridge to drain for 8–12 hours to remove the liquid; the longer you drain the labneh the thicker it will become. Remove the labneh from the cloth and transfer to an airtight container, then refrigerate for up to 7 days.

2   Preheat a fan-forced oven to 160°C.

3   Mix the oats, nuts and coconut, salt and cinnamon in a large bowl. Add the honey, vanilla and oil and mix until the dry ingredients are well coated. Spread the mixture onto a baking tray lined with baking paper and bake for 15–20 minutes or until golden. Stir occasionally to break up the lumps and rotate the tray to cook the granola evenly. Leave to cool for 10 minutes, then fold in the dried fruit.

4   Serve the granola with big pieces of watermelon, a dollop of the labneh, a drizzle of honey and a few sunflower seeds, if using.

Notes

- *Granola will keep for up to 4 days in an airtight container. Not only is it great for brekky with fresh fruit but it is also lovely sprinkled on ice cream.*

- *When the yoghurt is left to drain for a couple of days it becomes dry enough to roll into little balls, which can then be coated in chopped herbs or cracked pepper and drizzled with olive oil to serve as a snack or starter with flatbread.*

- *Labneh is also fantastic stirred into a tagine or stew at the last minute before serving.*

Toasted Corned Beef Sangers with Melted Cheese

When I lived in London I used to stop regularly on Finchley Road in Golders Green, a traditional Jewish area, and have a corned beef and rye sandwich piled high with sauerkraut. I still miss them. This recipe is based on my memory of these, in tandem with that New York classic, the Reuben sandwich. Make sure you use a great dense loaf of rye sourdough and cook the corned beef yourself – it will make all the difference.

1   Rinse the salted beef under cold running water. Place in a large saucepan with the celery, carrot, peppercorns, bay leaves and thyme, then cover with the water. Bring to the boil over high heat, then reduce the heat to low and simmer for 3 hours, topping up with extra water if required. Skim away any impurities. Remove the beef and set aside, then strain the stock. Store in an airtight container in the freezer for up to 2 months.

2   Combine the mayonnaise and dijon mustard in a small bowl and set aside.

3   Toast the bread under a hot griller, if desired, then spread with butter. Slice the beef and pile it high on 4 slices of the bread, then top with a slice of cheese. Add 2 tablespoons or so of sauerkraut to each sandwich. Place under the hot griller to melt the cheese slightly, then put another slice of bread on top.

4   Cut the sandwiches in half and serve with the mustard mayonnaise. Put a bag of salted potato crisps on the side, along with a bowl of dill pickles and caperberries (if using).

Notes

- Although you can use good-quality pastrami from your local deli, I prefer to a buy a piece of corned beef and cook it myself. Not only is it economical, it also tastes much better. You can get two or more meals out of the one piece of beef – corned beef and Home-style Mash (see page 188) for dinner and sandwiches the next day, and for the rest of the week, if you like.

- Cooking the beef in a crockpot works perfectly too, if you have one.

Serves 4

1 × 600 g piece corned salted beef brisket or silverside
1 small stick celery, roughly chopped
1 small carrot, roughly chopped
6 white peppercorns
2 fresh bay leaves
1 sprig thyme
2 litres water
80 ml Basic Mayonnaise (see page 181)
2 tablespoons dijon mustard
8 slices rye sourdough bread
butter, for spreading
4 slices gruyere cheese
1 cup sauerkraut
salted potato crisps, dill pickles and caperberries (optional), to serve

Caramelised Onion Tarts

Makes 4

50 ml olive oil
2 onions, thinly sliced
125 g caster sugar
3 teaspoons sherry vinegar
1 sheet prepared butter puff pastry
    (20 cm × 20 cm), thawed
30 g feta
1 handful rocket, washed and dried

Notes

- *Making caramel can be quite dangerous so you should take extra care, especially if there are children around. I recommend always having a small bowl of iced water next to a pan of bubbling caramel so if you accidentally burn yourself you can immediately plunge your hand into the iced water.*

- *Never leave a pan of caramel unattended on a hot stove as it can quickly overcook and burn.*

- *Professional kitchens have a copper pan specifically designed for boiling sugar with a spout for pouring the hot caramel. Copper pots are an excellent conductor of heat, which is why they are so highly valued.*

While these tarts make a great lunch, they are also perfect to offer as a little hand-around snack at parties. The secret is to make sure the onions are cooked slowly so they have a chance to soften and release all their lovely natural sugars. As a rule, the longer they cook, the sweeter they will be. Increase the heat at the end of cooking so they caramelise into a lovely deep amber-brown. A splash of good-quality sherry or red-wine vinegar at the end of cooking creates a sweet–sour note that is hard to resist.

1   Place the oil and onion in a heavy-based non-stick 28 cm frying pan over medium heat and cook, stirring occasionally, for 30 minutes or until the onion begins to colour and soften. The onion will continue to deepen in colour until you have a sweet caramelised mixture.

2   Meanwhile, heat the sugar in a small non-stick frying pan over high heat. When the sugar begins to melt around the edges, gently stir with a wooden spoon. As the sugar caramelises, do not stir it any further and remove it from the heat as soon as the caramel becomes a dark amber colour; this should take 3–4 minutes. Add the vinegar and swirl it into the caramel. Pour the caramel into four 9 cm × 4 cm soufflé dishes and leave to set for 15 minutes. Divide the caramelised onion between the dishes.

3   Preheat a fan-forced oven to 180°C.

4   Cut the pastry into four 9 cm rounds and pop them on top of the onion mixture. Place the dishes on a baking tray and bake for 20 minutes or until the pastry is fluffy and golden. Remove the tarts from the oven, then leave to stand for 2 minutes.

5   Invert the souffle dishes onto a platter or serving plates. Crumble a little feta over each tart and scatter with a few rocket leaves, then serve.

Crisp Parathas with Potato, Chilli and Coriander

My love of parathas was cemented during an extended stay in Singapore, a country that is a melting pot of Asian and European cultures. Indian influences can be seen in the delicious flatbreads that make up part of Singapore's culinary heritage – think roti, puri and chapatti, as well as, of course, parathas. They are a great spicy snack or light lunch which can be served either straight out of the pan or on a chopping board or a plate.

1   For the paratha bread, sift the flour and a pinch of salt into a bowl. Pour the milk into the flour, then add the melted butter and mix until the mixture comes together to form a soft dough. Tip the dough out onto a floured work surface, then knead until smooth, adding a little more flour if necessary to stop the dough from sticking. Transfer the dough to an oiled bowl, cover with plastic film and leave to rest for 30 minutes. Divide the dough into 8 small balls and roll each one out with a rolling pin to form 22 cm rounds, then set aside.

2   Meanwhile, place the potato in a small saucepan and cover with cold water. Bring to the boil and simmer for 15 minutes or until tender. Drain the potato and roughly crush with the back of a fork. Set aside to cool.

3   Add the chilli, ground cumin and coriander and half of the chopped coriander to the potato, then mix in. Spread the mixture between 4 of the pastry rounds. Cover each one with a remaining pastry round, then press down firmly with your fingers to seal the edge.

4   Heat the oil in a large heavy-based non-stick frying pan over medium heat. Gently place one paratha at a time in the pan and cook for 3 minutes on each side or until golden and crisp. Remove from the pan. Repeat with the remaining parathas.

5   Combine the cucumber, cherry tomatoes, pinch of salt and black sesame seeds. Blob some yoghurt over the parathas and scatter with the cucumber mixture and remaining coriander leaves, then serve with lime wedges.

Serves 4

2 potatoes, quartered
2 fresh long thin red chillies, finely chopped
1 teaspoon ground cumin
1 teaspoon ground coriander
⅓ cup roughly chopped coriander
vegetable oil, for cooking
1 cucumber, diced
250 g cherry tomatoes, halved
table salt
pinch of black sesame seeds
thick natural yoghurt and lime wedges, to serve

PARATHA BREAD
450 g plain flour, plus extra for dusting
table salt
375 ml milk
80 g unsalted butter, melted
30 ml olive oil

Notes

• *If you want to serve the unfilled parathas with a curry, such as my Lamb and Tomato Curry on page 96, roll the dough out into a single disc and fry it for a few minutes on each side until it is golden.*

• *Whole wheat or spelt flour can easily be substituted for white flour in this recipe.*

Gary's Can't-Eat-for-a-Week Burger with Onion Rings

Aim to buy freshly minced beef if you can. It's a good idea to get to know your local butcher and learn to trust his recommendations – if he is good he will be happy to mince some beef freshly just for you. You can always substitute minced lamb or chicken if you feel like a bit of a change. I also like to use grilled sourdough once in a while instead of soft burger buns, although there is definitely a place in my heart for both.

1 Cook the beetroot in a saucepan of simmering water for 40 minutes or until tender, then leave to cool. Peel and cut into 4 slices.

2 Heat a little of the olive oil in a frying pan over medium heat. Add the onion and garlic and cook for 2 minutes or until soft. Set aside to cool. Combine the mince with the onion and garlic, 1 teaspoon salt, a few grinds of pepper and the parsley, then form into 2 burger patties.

3 Preheat a barbecue grill-plate to medium, then grill the bread on both sides. Set aside and keep warm. Brush the patties with olive oil, then season with salt and pepper and grill on the barbecue for 4 minutes on each side or until cooked through. Meanwhile, grill the bacon. Place a slice of cheese on top of each patty and leave it to melt, then remove the patties and bacon from the grill. Keep warm.

4 For the onion rings, heat the oil in a deep heavy-based saucepan over high heat until it registers 185°C on a candy thermometer or until a cube of bread browns in 4–5 seconds. Reduce the heat to low. Dust the onion with flour and drop into the batter to coat, holding each ring above the batter to remove the excess. Slide the onion rings into the hot oil and fry for 3–4 minutes or until crisp and golden. Remove the onion rings with a slotted spoon and place on paper towel to drain. Sprinkle with sea salt.

5 Place a few lettuce leaves on the bases of the burger buns or 2 of the bread slices and top with the tomato, beetroot, patty and bacon, then finish with the tops of the burger buns or another slice of bread. Serve the burgers with a bowl of the tomato chutney and onion rings to the side.

Serves 2

1 beetroot
60 ml olive oil
½ small onion, finely chopped
1 clove garlic, chopped
500 g minced beef
table salt and freshly ground
    black pepper
2 tablespoons chopped flat-leaf
    parsley
2 soft burger buns, halved or
    4 slices sourdough bread
2 rashers bacon
2 slices cheddar cheese
½ baby cos lettuce, leaves separated
    or 2 inner iceberg lettuce leaves
1 large ox heart tomato, sliced
Tomato Chutney (see page 186),
    to serve

ONION RINGS
vegetable oil, for deep-frying
1 large onion, thickly sliced
50 g plain flour
½ quantity Beer Batter (see page 114)
sea salt

Notes

- *Remember that if you are using the barbecue to cook the burgers you don't want them encrusted with carbon or five-metre flames leaping in the air. Set the barbie on a medium flame and leave it to heat up, then brush the burgers with a little olive oil and place them on the grill-plate. You should then hear a gentle but definite sizzle, so easy does it!*

Japanese Pancake

These Japanese-style pancakes are called *okonomiyaki*, which means 'as you like it'. Real Japanese comfort food. My recipe is a slight variation on the original, and what makes it hard to resist is the slightly sweet and hot wasabi mayo and the sweet otafuki sauce. Delicious.

1 Place the potatoes in a small saucepan and cover with cold water. Bring to the boil and simmer for 15 minutes or until tender. When cool enough to handle, peel and slice, then set aside.

2 Meanwhile, mix the eggs in a bowl and season with the soy sauce, then set aside. Mix the mayonnaise with the wasabi and set aside.

3 Place the prawns, cabbage and mushrooms in a steamer basket over a pan of simmering water for 2 minutes.

4 Add the prawns, cabbage, mushrooms, potato, bean sprouts, tofu, water chestnuts and ginger to the egg mixture.

5 Heat a little peanut oil in a large heavy-based non-stick frying pan over high heat and pour in the batter. Cook the batter for 1 minute without stirring, then move it around a little and cook for another minute, then move the batter again. Place the pancake under a hot griller to cook for a further 3-4 minutes.

6 Transfer the pancake to a plate, then drizzle with the otafuki sauce and wasabi mayonnaise. Sprinkle with sesame seeds and coriander, then serve.

Notes

- *It is best to use a good-quality, heavy-based, non-stick frying pan, preferably one with a heat resistant handle so that it can be placed under the hot griller (handle and all) to finish cooking the pancake.*

- *Shifting the batter in the pan several times before placing it under the griller results in a fluffier pancake.*

- *You can vary the ingredients to utilise leftovers and whatever you happen to have in your fridge – some sweet potato and chopped spring onions or a little cooked chicken can be added for a delicious lunch or light dinner.*

Serves 4

2 kipfler potatoes, scrubbed
12 free-range eggs
1 tablespoon soy sauce
60 ml Basic Mayonnaise (see page 181)
2 teaspoons wasabi paste
(see page 197)
4 raw prawns, peeled
160 g Chinese cabbage, shredded
50 g fresh wood ear mushrooms, shredded
120 g bean sprouts
120 g soft tofu, cut into medium dice
100 g water chestnuts, quartered
30 g young ginger, thinly sliced
peanut oil, for pan-frying
otafuki sauce (see page 196), for drizzling
1 tablespoon toasted sesame seeds
coriander sprigs, to serve

Egg and Bacon Salad with Blue Cheese Dressing

This is my rendition of the more usual Caesar salad. It has been on the menu at Fenix and now The Boathouse on and off for ten years and continues to sell like hotcakes. Not that I dislike a nice Caesar, but it just doesn't do it for me. I personally think it needs bacon, and lots of fat, for it to taste gorgeous. The blue cheese dressing is the kicker for me – use a great blue cheese like stilton or gorgonzola piccante.

1 Preheat a fan-forced oven to 160°C.

2 Place the bacon on a baking tray lined with baking paper. Bake the bacon for 10 minutes or until golden and crisp. Set aside.

3 Drizzle the bread with olive oil, then place on the baking tray and toast in the oven for 7 minutes or until crisp and golden. Set aside.

4 Boil the eggs in a pan of simmering water for 8 minutes. Remove with a slotted spoon and cool under cold running water. Remove the shells. Dry the eggs with paper towel and roughly chop. Set aside.

5 Spoon a little dressing over a serving plate or platter and place the lettuce on top. Spoon a little more dressing over the lettuce, then scatter with the egg, bread, blue cheese and bacon. Season with salt and pepper and serve.

Serves 4

4 rashers bacon, rind removed, finely chopped
4 slices dense sourdough bread, cut into 5 mm dice
50 ml extra virgin olive oil
2 free-range eggs
200 ml Blue Cheese Dressing (see page 181)
3 baby cos lettuces, outer leaves discarded, halved lengthways and carefully washed and dried
100 g blue cheese, such as gorgonzola piccante, crumbled
sea salt flakes and freshly ground white pepper

Notes
- *Make sure you remove your eggs from the fridge well before you boil them. The eggs should be at room temperature as this prevents the shells from cracking due to the dramatic temperature change when fridge-cold eggs hit boiling water.*

Club Sandwich

I love a good club sandwich – in fact, if I am staying in a hotel anywhere in the world I find it's normally the safest bet from room service, especially after midnight! The whole bacon, lettuce and tomato thing, combined with the chicken and egg thing, put together with crisp toast – how perfect. It's also good for a light lunch using leftover chook from the Sunday roast. There is no secret to a good club sandwich other than making it with care, which means using fresh bread and good-quality ingredients. The thing that makes the real difference is the build – get everything ready and construct the layers carefully – then hold on boys!

1   Preheat a chargrill pan or barbecue grill-plate. Drizzle the chicken with a little of the olive oil, then sprinkle with salt, pepper and a little lemon zest. Set aside.

2   Boil the eggs in a pan of simmering water for 9 minutes. Cool under cold running water, then shell and slice.

3   Grill the bacon until it is crisp. Grill the chicken for 8–10 minutes or until tinged golden, then drain on paper towel and keep warm.

4   Meanwhile, chargrill or toast the bread and keep warm. Mix the mayonnaise with the mustard, then add the lettuce and season with salt and pepper.

5   Lay the bread out in two rows, spread with butter, then place the lettuce mixture on 4 of the slices and spread evenly. Lay the egg and chicken on the first slice and the tomato and bacon on the second.

6   Stack the egg and chicken layer over the tomato and bacon layer to make 2 club sandwiches, then cover with the last 2 bread slices. Press down to hold and cut in half. Serve with pickles and – my preference – potato crisps.

Serves 2

1 chicken breast fillet, thinly sliced
extra virgin olive oil
sea salt flakes and freshly
    ground black pepper
finely grated lemon zest, for
    sprinkling
2 free-range eggs
2 rashers bacon
6 slices good-quality bread,
    such as sourdough or ciabatta
80 ml Basic Mayonnaise (see page 181)
1 teaspoon wholegrain mustard
¼ head crisp iceberg lettuce,
    finely shredded
40 g unsalted butter
1 ripe ox heart tomato, thinly sliced
potato crisps and dill pickles
    (optional), to serve

Notes

- *Make sure you remove your eggs from the fridge well before you boil them. The eggs should be at room temperature as this prevents the shells from cracking due to the dramatic temperature change when fridge-cold eggs hit boiling water.*

- *While it is up to you, I suggest being generous with the mayo as it tastes fabulous. The bread you use is also critical to a great sanger. I prefer to use either an open-textured sourdough or sourdough rye.*

- *The chicken and bacon can easily be pan-fried, if preferred.*

Cheese Pies

Don't underestimate the importance of a good-quality butter puff pastry – it will make all the difference to this recipe. There are a couple of excellent brands on the market now that are available from good delis and food stores – look out for Carême if you can find it. A good local bakery may also sell you puff pastry, but failing all of that, this recipe will also work with filo (see Notes).

Makes 12

vegetable oil spray, for greasing
4 sheets prepared butter puff pastry (20 cm × 20 cm), thawed
2 × 200 g rolls hard goat's cheese, evenly cut into 6 slices each
12 slices flat pancetta
2 sprigs thyme, leaves picked

1   Preheat a fan-forced oven to 100°C.

2   Lightly spray the holes of a 12-hole capacity muffin tray with oil.

3   Cut the puff pastry into twelve 5 cm × 5 cm squares. Gently push the pastry into the muffin holes. Wrap each cheese round with a slice of pancetta and place it in the centre of a pastry cup. Sprinkle each one with some thyme, then pinch the pastry in 4 'corners' around the cheese; you should still be able to see the cheese (see opposite). Bake the pies for 10–15 minutes.

4   Cool the pies a little in the tray, then turn them out and serve warm.

Notes
- *To use filo pastry, brush 5–6 sheets with a little oil, then layer them in the muffin holes. Lightly brown in the oven before adding the pancetta-wrapped cheese and thyme for a final blast to render the cheese gooey.*

- *As well as soft fresh goat's cheese, which is now widely available in larger supermarkets, you can purchase a range of aged goat's cheeses that differ in texture, density and, of course, flavour. I encourage you to try them to find one you like best.*

- *Goat's milk cheese is very high in protein and often people who can't tolerate cow's milk and cow's milk products find they don't have the same issue with goat's milk.*

- *To make 6 larger pies, grease a 6-hole capacity muffin tray, then cut the pastry into six 10 cm × 10 cm squares and cut the cheese into 6 slices. Proceed with the recipe.*

Stir-fried Broken Rice with Chinese Sausage

This recipe has developed over the years and I think it includes just about all of my favourite ingredients. It has no specific place of origin, being a little Indonesian, a little Japanese and a little Chinese. Oh – and the broken rice, is of course, Vietnamese. I am not fussed because it tastes great. Please don't feel that you need to use all of the ingredients; perhaps just start with the egg, garlic and Chinese broccoli, then sprinkle in the dashi powder (it adds a bit of a kick), then throw in some bean sprouts and leave it at that.

1   Place the rice in a small saucepan and rinse under cold water, then drain – repeat 3 times. Cover with the water and add a pinch of salt, then bring to the boil over medium heat. Reduce the heat to low, then cover and simmer for 15 minutes or until the liquid has been absorbed by the rice. Turn off the heat and leave to stand for 15 minutes. Spread the rice onto a tray and leave to cool and dry in the fridge for 6 hours, if you have the time.

2   Bring the sugar and vinegar to the boil in a small saucepan, then add the ginger and simmer over low heat for 5 minutes. Remove from the heat and set aside.

3   Heat the peanut oil in a wok over medium heat. Deep-fry two-thirds of the shallot until golden and crisp, then remove with a slotted spoon and drain on paper towel, then repeat with two-thirds of the garlic. Set aside.

4   Put the sausage and tempeh into the wok and fry for 2 minutes. Add the Chinese broccoli and cook for a further 2 minutes. Remove and set aside. Put the chilli and remaining shallot and garlic into the wok and fry for 1 minute to release the aroma. Add the egg, stirring as it cooks. Add the rice and increase the heat to high. Stir-fry the mixture for 2–3 minutes, charring the rice slightly. Return the sausage, tempeh and Chinese broccoli to the wok. Season with a pinch of dashi and splash of soy, then add some of the coriander and spring onion, along with the bean sprouts.

5   Scatter the rice with the crisp shallots and garlic, remaining coriander, spring onion and the drained candied ginger. Serve with lime wedges to the side.

Serves 4

200 g broken rice (see page 194)
400 ml water
table salt
75 g caster sugar
80 ml coconut vinegar (see page 195)
1 knob young ginger, thinly sliced
60 ml peanut oil
6 shallots, thinly sliced
1 head garlic, thinly sliced
120 g Chinese sausage, sliced (see page 194)
200 g tempeh (see page 197)
1 bunch Chinese broccoli, trimmed and shredded
2 fresh small red chillies, shredded
1 free-range egg
pinch of dashi powder (see page 195)
dash of mushroom soy sauce
¼ cup coriander leaves
4 spring onions, chopped
2 handfuls bean sprouts
lime wedges, to serve

Notes:

- *I am a big fan of broken rice and love its texture when just steamed or charred in a wok. I prefer to dry out the cooked rice in the fridge before frying, so if you want to do this you'll need to cook it at least 6 hours in advance of when you wish to serve it.*

- *Frying your own shallots and garlic will give this fragrant rice dish a beautiful touch of freshness. However, you can also purchase readymade crisp-fried shallots and garlic in plastic containers from Asian food stores.*

Cauliflower Cheese with Pangrattato

Serves 6

200 ml milk
20 g unsalted butter
20 g plain flour
40 g tasty cheese, grated
1.5 litres water
table salt
1 small cauliflower, trimmed,
    cut into florets
50 ml pouring cream
1 free-range egg yolk
70 g grated Parmigiano Reggiano
3 tablespoons Pangrattato
    (see page 188)

Notes

• Making the perfect white sauce is more about understanding how heat works than whisking the sauce until it is smooth. Make sure the milk is hot before adding it to the roux and stir it in a little at a time, then bring the sauce to the boil. As the sauce starts to thicken, stir until it is super-smooth, before adding more hot milk.

• If both the cauliflower and white sauce are hot then you can place the dish under a hot griller until the top is golden brown rather than baking it in the oven.

Cauliflower cheese reminds me of my childhood. Mum would make it all the time, presumably because I was an awkward eater and slathering the cauliflower in white sauce and cheddar would do the trick. The crunchy breadcrumbs (*pangrattato*, in Italian) are all about texture, and offer a great crunchy contrast to the soft cauliflower and oozy white sauce. If you want to make it extra-special, then a scattering of crumbled smoky bacon sets it all off brilliantly.

1   Bring the milk to the boil in a saucepan over high heat, then remove it from the heat. Meanwhile, melt the butter in another saucepan over medium heat. Add the flour and stir for 2–3 minutes or until white tinges appear on the flour and butter mixture (this is called a roux). Add 1 ladleful of the hot milk at a time to the roux. Before adding more hot milk, stir the mixture until it is smooth. Reduce the heat to low and cook the sauce for another 5–6 minutes, stirring regularly to prevent the mixture from sticking. Remove from the heat and add the grated cheese, then stir in to melt. Set aside.

2   Preheat a fan-forced oven to 180°C.

3   Bring the water to the boil in a large saucepan and add a pinch of salt. Cook the cauliflower for 5 minutes or until just tender. Remove the cauliflower, then drain thoroughly for 1–2 minutes to ensure it is completely dry. Arrange it in a baking dish with the florets facing upwards.

4   Whip the cream with a whisk. Mix the egg yolk into the cheese sauce, then fold in the whipped cream and parmesan. Spoon the sauce over the cauliflower so it is covered, then sprinkle with the pangrattato.

5   Bake for 10 minutes or until bubbly and golden brown. Serve immediately.

Leek, Anchovy and Onion Pies

This southern Italian recipe comes from a long family tradition: it is brought to other families as gifts during festival seasons and enjoyed warm or at room temperature. Thanks to the mum of The Boathouse chef Angelo Sanfillipo for this recipe. It is a staple at her family table, and now makes a regular appearance on The Boathouse menu too.

1   For the olive oil dough, place the flour, salt and gluten into a large mixing bowl. Make a well in the centre. Dissolve the yeast in the warm water and pour into the flour mixture, then add the olive oil. With your hands, work the wet ingredients into the dry ingredients until they come together to form a dough. Knead until smooth, then transfer to a lightly oiled bowl, cover with a tea towel or plastic film and set aside in a warm place. Leave for 1 hour or until doubled in size.

2   Meanwhile, slice the leeks in half down the centre, then wash well and roughly chop. Place a splash of olive oil in a deep saucepan, then cook the leek over medium heat for 5 minutes or until it begins to soften (the green part will take the longest). Drain and set aside.

3   Preheat a fan-forced oven to 200°C.

4   Sweat the anchovy fillets and onion in a frying pan over medium heat for 5 minutes, then add the pepper to incorporate the flavours as much as possible. Add the leek and set aside.

5   Roll the dough, then divide into four 140 g balls, cover with a tea towel or plastic film and leave to prove again for 30 minutes or until doubled in size. The second time won't take as long as the yeast has already been activated.

6   Stretch the dough balls out to form four 24 cm rounds. Divide the filling into quarters. Place one-quarter of the leek mixture on one side of the dough, leaving a 1 cm border to allow the dough to seal when it is folded over. Fold over the other side of the dough to enclose the filling, then push the edges down, using a little oil to help seal the dough. Fold the edge over your index finger to create a crimped edge, then brush with a little olive oil. Sprinkle with a little salt.

7   Bake the pies for 15–20 minutes or until golden brown. Slice or leave whole and serve warm or at room temperature.

Serves 4

1 bunch leeks, trimmed
olive oil, for cooking
100 g anchovy fillets
2 white onions, thinly sliced
2 teaspoons freshly ground
    black pepper
sea salt flakes

OLIVE OIL DOUGH
550 g plain flour, plus extra
    for dusting
30 g table salt
30 g gluten (see page 196)
20 g fresh yeast
320 ml warm water
100 ml extra virgin olive oil

Notes

- *The mixture of plain flour and yeast allows the dough to rise; however, it creates a dense and tight dough which is what we are looking for in this particular recipe.*

Chicken and White Bean Soup

A good chicken soup is the ultimate pick-me-up, and easily makes the transition between winter and summer, with a few adjustments here and there. Poaching a whole chicken first results in a brilliant stock, circumventing the need to use shoddy, pre-made stuff. The chicken and stock are the essence of this soup, so feel free to vary the vegetables from season to season, and to replace the beans with a grain such as rice, barley or freekah.

1   Place the chicken in a large saucepan or stockpot and cover with the stock and water, then add the cannellini beans and bring to a gentle simmer over medium heat. Add the bay leaf and thyme, then cook over low heat for 50 minutes or until the chicken is cooked and the beans are tender. Remove from the heat and leave to stand for 15 minutes. Remove the chicken and beans from the stock and set aside. Strain the stock and reserve. When the chicken is cool enough to handle, remove the skin and shred the meat from the bones into bite-sized pieces. Set aside.

2   Meanwhile, rinse the pan and return it to the stove. Heat the olive oil over medium heat, then add the garlic and fry for 30 seconds or until golden. Add the carrot, onion and celery and cook for a further 2–3 minutes. Return the stock, beans and chicken to the pan and bring to the boil, then simmer for 10 minutes. Add the black cabbage and beans and cook for a further 3 minutes, then add the peas and cook for another 1 minute. Season to taste with salt and pepper.

3   Ladle the soup into bowls, then drizzle with extra virgin olive oil and serve with chargrilled sourdough to the side.

Notes
- *When cooking dried cannellini beans I rinse them well first as they can be quite dirty. I don't soak them (or other softer category dried beans such as lentils and split peas) before cooking.*

- *I don't add salt to the pan of cooking beans as this toughens them. Instead, season them at the end of cooking.*

- *If you can't find Tuscan black cabbage, then use shredded silverbeet or kale instead.*

Serves 4

1 × 1.25 kg free-range chicken
1 litre Chicken Stock (see page 183)
500 ml water
150 g dried cannellini beans, well washed and drained
1 fresh bay leaf
2 sprigs thyme
70 ml extra virgin olive oil, plus extra for drizzling
2 cloves garlic, finely chopped
1 carrot, finely chopped
1 onion, finely chopped
2 sticks celery, finely chopped
1 bunch Tuscan black cabbage (cavolo nero), washed and roughly shredded
1 handful green beans, trimmed, sliced
1 cup frozen or fresh peas
sea salt flakes and freshly ground black pepper
chargrilled sourdough bread, to serve

Brandade with Capsicum Confit

Throughout history, cod has been an all-powerful commodity. In the sixteenth and seventeenth centuries, the Atlantic North Sea was fished for cod, which was then salted and preserved. Cod underpinned much of the trade between the developing economies of Spain, Portugal, England, France and Scandinavia. Salt cod-based dishes such as French brandade and Spanish baccala crop up all over Europe. Today, fish fingers and crumbed fish have devastated cod stocks. While brandade is traditionally made with salt cod, I use fresh blue-eye trevalla that I salt in the fridge overnight.

1 Sprinkle half of the rock salt onto a plate, then place the fish on top and sprinkle with the remaining rock salt. Cover with plastic film and leave in the fridge overnight.

2 Preheat a fan-forced oven to 160°C.

3 Place the potato directly on an oven shelf and bake for 45 minutes or until soft. Scoop out the flesh and set aside next to the stove to keep warm.

4 Meanwhile, for the capsicum confit, place the capsicums on a sheet of foil on a baking tray, then drizzle with the olive oil and sprinkle with garlic. Draw up the sides of foil to enclose, then place in the oven with the potato for 30 minutes. Remove the capsicums and cool for 10 minutes. Cut the capsicums in half, then discard the seeds and cut the flesh lengthways into rough pieces. Transfer to a serving bowl and pour over the oily roasting juices, then set aside.

5 Rinse the fish of salt, then pat dry with paper towel. Place in a heavy-based saucepan. Add the milk, thyme, bay leaves and peppercorns. Bring to a gentle simmer over medium heat, then cook for 3–4 minutes. Drain the fish, discarding the herbs and peppercorns and reserving 50 ml of the strained milk. Crumble the fish finely between your fingers.

6 Heat half of the olive oil in a heavy-based saucepan over low heat, then add the garlic and whisk until fragrant for 1 minute. Add the fish and continue whisking over the heat until the oil has been absorbed. Gradually add the remaining olive oil. Add the potato, then the reserved milk and whisk vigorously until creamy. Remove from the heat and whisk in the cream.

7 Serve the warm brandade with the sourdough or brioche and the capsicum confit to the side.

Serves 4–6

30 g rock salt
1 × 180 g blue-eye trevalla fillet, skin removed, pin-boned, patted dry
1 potato
250 ml milk
2 sprigs thyme
2 fresh bay leaves
½ teaspoon white peppercorns
50 ml extra virgin olive oil
1½ cloves garlic, crushed
50 ml pouring cream
chargrilled or toasted sourdough bread or brioche, to serve

CAPSICUM CONFIT
2 red capsicums
3 teaspoons olive oil
½ clove garlic, sliced

Notes

- *Reduce the time allocated for salting the fish if you wish to save a few hours, depending on how salty you like the fish to be. I prefer to salt it longer because it draws out moisture, intensifying the flavour and reducing the weight of the fish.*

- *I use new-season potatoes (see page 196) for brandade as they give it the softest, fluffiest texture. As potatoes get older their sugar content increases and their texture changes. They can become gluey when mashed and their flavour is not the best.*

- *Leftover brandade can be stored in an airtight container in the fridge for up to 5 days.*

Chicken Liver Parfait with Toast

Serves 10

250 g chicken livers
250 ml milk
2 tablespoons olive oil
6 shallots, thinly sliced
1 clove garlic
50 ml Madeira
100 ml port
50 ml brandy
3 free-range eggs
1½ teaspoons table salt
½ teaspoon freshly ground
    white pepper
250 g unsalted butter, at room
    temperature, chopped
boiling water, for cooking
melted butter, to seal
Grape, Ginger and Mustard Chutney,
    to serve (see page 186)

TOAST
1 sourdough ficelle (small baguette),
    thinly sliced lengthways
melted butter, for brushing
sea salt flakes

Notes

- *Parfait is not the easiest recipe to perfect. However, you will go a long way to achieving success if you pay attention to the temperature of both the butter and liver puree and ensure that you cook the mixture in a water bath at precisely 120°C.*

- *Buy a good-quality meat thermometer to add to your stash of kitchen gadgets. It is useful to have on hand at times when it is important to test the internal temperature of dishes such as this parfait or a terrine (they should reach 60°C in the centre) as this will confirm that it is time to remove the dish from the oven.*

I have tried many chicken liver pate or parfait recipes in my time but this is the best – silky-smooth and packed with flavour. It's very rich so have just a little at a time and savour. Buy super-fresh chicken livers and make sure you trim off all the connective tissue. You'll need to get started on this the day before you wish to serve it.

1   To clean the chicken livers, remove the little pieces of sinew in the middle of each one. Rinse the livers under cold water and soak in the milk in the fridge overnight.

2   Heat the olive oil in a saucepan over low heat. Fry the shallot for a few seconds. Add the garlic, Madeira, port and brandy and cook over low heat for another 3–4 minutes or until reduced by two-thirds. Set aside to cool.

3   Preheat a fan-forced oven to 180°C.

4   For the toast, brush the sourdough slices with a little butter, then sprinkle with salt. Place on a baking tray and bake for 4–5 minutes or until golden. Leave to cool and set aside.

5   Drain the chicken livers and blend in a food processor until smooth. Add the eggs and blend to incorporate, then add the shallot reduction and season with the salt and pepper.

6   Place the butter in a large heatproof bowl. (The butter must be very soft – almost melting – as it is important that the butter and liver puree are at the same temperature, otherwise the butter will curdle the mixture as it stiffens. To test, dip your index finger into the butter and then into the liver puree.) Add the puree to the butter and whisk it through until the mixture reaches a rich and smooth consistency. If the butter sets or curdles the mixture, warm it very gently over a pan of simmering water over low heat, whisking continuously until it smooths out.

7   Preheat the fan-forced oven to 120°C.

8   Divide the mixture among two 500 ml-capacity airtight glass jars. Place the jars in a deep baking dish or roasting pan and fill with enough hot water to reach halfway up the side of the jars. Cook in the oven for 45 minutes or until the parfait has set. (If you have a meat thermometer, the internal temperature should register 60°C.)

9   Remove the jars from the oven, then pour a 2–3 mm-deep layer of melted butter over the top of each parfait to seal. Seal the jars, then leave to cool and place in the fridge. Serve the parfait with the toast and chutney. Once the seal is broken, the parfait will keep in the fridge for 4–5 days.

Shredded Fennel and Cabbage Salad with Parmesan

Serves 4

1 small savoy cabbage, outer leaves
    and base trimmed, inner leaves
    very finely shredded
1 bulb fennel, finely shredded
50 ml white balsamic vinegar
150 ml extra virgin olive oil
sea salt flakes
80 g Parmigiano Regianno, grated
50 ml aged balsamic vinegar
freshly ground white pepper

As with all salad ingredients, fresh is best so make this salad in winter, when fennel and savoy cabbage are at their seasonal peak. You need to make sure that you shred the cabbage and fennel as finely as possible using a knife or mandoline as this results in a delicate salad that is beautiful to eat.

1   Combine the cabbage and fennel in a large bowl and dress with the white balsamic and olive oil. Add a pinch of salt and 60 g of the Parmigiano and mix gently.

2   Mound the salad onto plates, then drizzle with aged balsamic, sprinkle with the remaining Parmigiano, season with pepper and serve.

Notes

- Apparently there is no difference between so-called 'male' (longer and thinner) or 'female' (plumper and rounder) fennel, so just buy plump fennel bulbs with their fronds still attached.

- Using a mandoline makes it easier to shred the fennel and cabbage finely.

- For best results, toss the dressing and Parmigiano through the salad at the last minute before serving.

Ocean Trout, Pancetta and Watercress Salad

Trout, pancetta and watercress is a match made in heaven – it speaks to me of rivers and hedgerows and Hampshire, which is where I was born in the UK. Horseradish is as English as can be and should not just be reserved for serving with roast beef on a Sunday – it also works brilliantly with fish. The best watercress in the UK is grown in Hampshire, so when I eat this dish I think of the rolling green hills of the South Downs. A culinary trip down memory lane is good for the soul every once in a while!

1   Preheat a fan-forced oven to 60°C (if you do not have a digital oven, set it on the lowest temperature and leave the door ajar).

2   Cook the potatoes in boiling salted water until just tender, then peel and set aside to cool.

3   Meanwhile, bake the pancetta on a baking tray lined with baking paper for 6 minutes or until crisp. Break into large pieces and set aside.

4   For the horseradish cream, mix the horseradish and vinegar in a small bowl, then leave to stand for 5 minutes. Mix in the crème fraîche.

5   Sprinkle the trout with 2 teaspoons of the olive oil and bake in the oven for 20 minutes or until just cooked and still opaque.

6   Mix the remaining olive oil and hazelnut oil with the lemon zest and juice. Set aside.

7   Place the radish and watercress in a large bowl. Slice the potatoes into 1 cm-thick rounds, then add to the bowl. Drizzle a little of the vinaigrette over the potato, then add a pinch of salt and a twist of pepper. Set aside.

8   Cut the trout into neat bite-sized pieces. Spoon a generous amount of the horseradish cream onto 4 plates, then divide the trout, potato, radish and pancetta between the plates and scatter with the watercress. Drizzle a little more of the vinaigrette around the edge of the horseradish cream, then serve with the remaining horseradish cream alongside.

Serves 4

4 kipfler potatoes
table salt
4 thin slices flat pancetta
400 g ocean trout fillets, skinned and pin-boned
60 ml olive oil
50 ml hazelnut oil (see page 196)
finely grated zest and juice of 1 lemon
6 radishes, trimmed, thinly sliced
1 handful small watercress sprigs
freshly ground white pepper

HORSERADISH CREAM
1 tablespoon freshly grated horseradish
2 teaspoons champagne vinegar
250 ml crème fraîche

Notes

· *Ocean trout, like salmon, should be cooked until still pink in the centre for best results. The beauty of slow cooking these fish is that they will appear to be almost raw, however, the texture will have changed and the flesh will be pale and almost translucent. If you don't feel comfortable with cooking fish this way then feel free to cook it quickly on the barbecue or flash-fry it in a heavy-based non-stick frying pan – please don't overcook it or the fish will be spoilt.*

· *Ocean trout tends to be cheaper than salmon, plus it is jam-packed with Omega 3 fatty acids.*

Pasta, Pizza and Risotto

Spaghetti and Meatballs

I love this recipe because as my daughter was growing up, we fed her vegetables in these meatballs and she never knew it. Funny thing was that we liked it too. As every parent knows, adding grated zucchini or carrot doesn't always work – the kids find it no matter how small. So make a batch of carrot (as I've done here), sweet potato or cauliflower puree and pop it in zip-lock bags in the freezer for when you need it. Instead of using egg to bind the meatballs, replace it with the puree. The result is soft, sweet and delicious meatballs that are nutritious too! Although it may not always be popular with the kids, freshly chopped parsley, oregano or tarragon is a nice addition at the end of cooking.

1   Cook the carrot, butter and water in a covered saucepan over low heat, stirring occasionally, for 10 minutes or until the carrot is soft (cooking under a tight-fitting lid helps the carrot to cook quickly). Puree in a small food processor, then set aside to cool.

2   Mix the minced veal and pork, breadcrumbs, carrot puree and parsley (if using) in a large bowl. Season with 1 teaspoon salt and a little pepper and mould into 2 cm meatballs; you should have 24 meatballs. Set aside.

3   Preheat a fan-forced oven to 165°C.

4   Heat the olive oil in a large ovenproof non-stick saucepan or enamelled cast-iron casserole. Brown the meatballs over high heat until golden on all sides, then remove and set aside. Fry the onion and garlic for 1 minute or until translucent and soft, then add the tomato paste, tomato and stock. Return the meatballs to the pan, then add the thyme, bay leaves and a little salt and pepper. Bring to a gentle simmer over medium heat, then cover. Cook in the oven for 45 minutes, gently stirring occasionally.

5   Meanwhile, cook the spaghetti following packet instructions in a saucepan of boiling salted water until al dente. Drain. Serve the meatballs with the spaghetti and plenty of grated pecorino.

Serves 4

1 small carrot, finely grated
30 g unsalted butter
100 ml water
400 g minced veal
400 g minced pork
100 g fresh breadcrumbs
¼ cup chopped flat-leaf parsley (optional)
table salt and freshly ground white pepper
60 ml extra virgin olive oil
1 onion, finely chopped
2 cloves garlic, chopped
2 tablespoons tomato paste
2 × 400 g tins chopped tomato
100 ml Chicken Stock (see page 183)
2 sprigs thyme
2 fresh bay leaves
320 g spaghetti
grated pecorino, to serve

Notes

- *This recipe suits the pressure cooker. Fry the meatballs in a heavy-based non-stick frying pan until golden all over as this adds both colour and flavour. Meanwhile, make the sauce in the pressure cooker, then add the meatballs, stir and pop on the lid. Once pressure is reached, turn the heat down to low and cook for 15 minutes. Perfect results and quick too as the meatballs taste as though they have been cooked for an hour.*

- *I often add 1 tablespoon smoked paprika (see page 197) and 1 teaspoon chilli flakes to the onion before adding the tomato. I then stir through 1 tablespoon chopped coriander just before serving with rice or couscous.*

Semolina Gnocchi with Gorgonzola

I love semolina gnocchi. Although it is not trendy, it deserves more airplay. It's light and easy to make and, because the semolina needs to be chilled, it makes a great 'leftover' meal that can be fried, baked or grilled.

1   Grease a baking dish or cake tin (about 25 cm × 25 cm × 5 cm deep).

2   Bring the milk, salt and grated nutmeg to the boil in a saucepan over high heat. Gradually sprinkle in the semolina, whisking it through. Cook for 10–15 minutes over low heat, stirring regularly to prevent sticking. Remove from the heat and add the egg yolk and Parmigiano, then quickly stir through to mix. Spread the semolina mixture evenly into the prepared dish. Cover with plastic film and place in the fridge for 1 hour or until firm.

3   Preheat a fan-forced oven to 165°C.

4   Blend the mascarpone with 70 g of the gorgonzola in a food processor, then add a few grinds of pepper. Add the lemon zest and juice and blend to mix. Set aside.

5   Spread the bread on a baking tray, then drizzle with the olive oil. Toast in the oven for 10 minutes or until golden. Cool and crush roughly. Set aside.

6   Cut the semolina mixture into circles or squares and place in a baking dish, then top each one with a dollop of the mascarpone mixture. Crumble over the remaining gorgonzola, then grill under a hot griller until it bubbles. Sprinkle with the breadcrumbs and return to the griller for 30 seconds or until golden brown. Serve immediately.

Serves 4

550 ml milk
½ teaspoon table salt
3–4 grates fresh nutmeg
100 g semolina
1 free-range egg yolk
30 g freshly grated Parmigiano Regianno
110 g mascarpone
100 g gorgonzola
freshly ground white pepper
finely grated zest and juice of ½ lemon
60 g brioche or dense sourdough bread, torn into small pieces
1 tablespoon extra virgin olive oil

Notes

· *Gnocchi is simple to make and cheap to boot. It is great served as an entree, light meal or side dish. Try it with a nice fresh tomato sauce and a grating of good Italian cheese.*

Gnocchi with Oxtail Bolognese

Serves 4

1 × 1 kg oxtail, fat trimmed, cut
    into pieces between the joints
50 g plain flour
table salt and freshly ground
    white pepper
90 ml extra virgin olive oil
300 g minced veal
300 g minced pork
1 onion, finely chopped
2 cloves garlic, chopped
2 carrots, grated
60 ml tomato paste
2 × 400 g tins chopped tomato
1 litre Beef or Veal Stock
    (see page 182)
2 sprigs thyme
2 fresh bay leaves
2 tablespoons chopped flat-leaf
    parsley
grated pecorino, to serve

GNOCCHI
1 kg new-season potatoes
    (see page 196), such as sebago
table salt and freshly ground
    white pepper
1 free-range egg
250 g plain flour, plus extra
    for dusting

Notes

- *To make great gnocchi it is important to start with fluffy potatoes. The trouble with recommending specific cultivars is that the sugar content of individual potatoes changes as they get older, so use new-season potatoes. Ask your greengrocer for a good baking potato.*

- *If you knead the dough too much it develops the gluten in the flour and you run the risk of the gnocchi becoming heavy and chewy. Handle the dough gently and press it down as described opposite.*

I have made so many versions of this classic sauce, but this is my all-time favourite. It does take a little longer than usual, but the oxtail adds a complexity. Who gave this recipe to me? Well, it was a good friend's dad – a proud Italian cook, so he must be right. Make a batch, then transfer it to zip-lock bags and freeze it for emergencies. While I've chosen to serve it with gnocchi here, it is also perfect with pasta such as spaghetti or rigatoni.

1   Preheat a fan-forced oven to 160°C.

2   Dust the oxtail with flour and season with salt and pepper. Heat the oil in a large ovenproof saucepan or enamelled cast-iron casserole over high heat. Add the oxtail and fry until golden on all sides. Remove and set aside.

3   Add the minced veal and pork to the pan and fry for 4 minutes or until it starts to brown, then season with salt and pepper. Add the onion and garlic and cook for a further 3–4 minutes or until they soften. Add the carrot, tomato paste, tomato and stock. Return the oxtail to the pan, then add the thyme, bay leaves and a little pepper. Bring to a simmer and pop a lid on, then cook in the oven for 2½ hours.

4   Remove the oxtail and pick off the meat, discarding the bones and returning the meat to the pan. Add the parsley to the bolognese and set aside.

5   For the gnocchi, increase the oven temperature to 180°C. Bake the potatoes for 45 minutes (or boil them in their skins for 20 minutes or until soft). Peel the hot potatoes and immediately press through a potato ricer or push through a sieve over a bowl. Season the potato with 3 teaspoons salt and a little pepper and mix through the egg. Sprinkle half of the flour onto a bench and place the potato mixture on top. Flatten the mixture until it is 4 cm thick, then sprinkle with the remaining flour. Press the mixture down with your fingers, then fold it over. Repeat this process until all the flour has been incorporated.

6   Bring a large saucepan of water to the boil over high heat, then add a good pinch of salt. Meanwhile, gather the dough together to form a ball. When you press your finger into the dough it should just spring back or have a touch of resistance. Dust the bench with a little extra flour, then divide the dough into quarters. Roll each quarter into a long sausage-shape using liberal amounts of flour to dust. Cut into little pillow shapes (gnocchi) about 2 cm long. Gently place the gnocchi in the boiling water; when they rise to the surface they are cooked. To test, remove 1 gnocchi from the water and taste; it should be soft and yielding, not chewy. Remove the gnocchi from the pan with a slotted spoon, then season with a pinch of salt.

7   Heat the bolognese to warm through, then serve with the gnocchi and plenty of grated pecorino.

Linguine with Fresh Tuna, Chilli and Garlic

This is one of the simplest pasta dishes you can make. Much like the classic garlic, chilli and parsley sauce, *aglio e olio*, this one relies on browning garlic and dissolving anchovies in oil to create the flavour base. It's a powerful combination, infused with anchovies, which are nature's own stock cubes and not at all fishy when used in this way. For many years I underestimated the flavour of a simple sauce combined in the pan with good-quality pasta and extra virgin olive oil. The pasta continues to cook in the sauce, soaking up all the lovely pan flavours.

1   Cook the pasta in a large saucepan of boiling salted water for 6–8 minutes or until al dente; stir gently during the first couple of minutes to make sure the pasta doesn't stick together.

2   Meanwhile, heat a deep heavy-based non-stick frying pan or saute pan over medium heat, then pour in half of the olive oil. Add the garlic, chilli and anchovy and cook for 2 minutes or until the garlic browns and the anchovy begins to break up. Add the wine, then bring to the boil and simmer for 2 minutes or until the mixture has reduced by half.

3   Drain the pasta reserving a little of the cooking water. Tip the pasta into the pan of hot sauce. Add the tuna, lemon zest, juice, rocket and remaining olive oil. Season well with salt and pepper and toss well to mix, adding the reserved pasta water if desired. Sprinkle in half of the pangrattato, then stir once or twice and divide between 4 bowls. Sprinkle with the remaining pangrattato and serve.

Notes

- *When cooking pasta, remember that adding oil to the pan of boiling water is an old wives' tale! It makes the pasta slippery so the sauce slides off it rather than adheres to it. Plenty of boiling salted water is all that is required to cook great pasta. Stir at the start to prevent sticking and cook until it is firm to the bite but not chalky, that is, al dente.*

- *Never rinse cooked pasta under running water; simply drain, sprinkle with a little olive oil to keep it separate after cooking, then season with sea salt flakes and leave it to cool in the open air, if desired.*

- *This dish needs a meaty fish such as a game fish like tuna, swordfish or marlin. The secret to its success is to cook the fish quickly, leaving it pink and moist in the centre – here the tuna is cooked by the residual heat of the pasta and sauce. Overcook it and the fish will be dry and lack the soft texture that you want here.*

Serves 4

500 g dried linguine
table salt
100 ml extra virgin olive oil
2 cloves garlic, sliced
4 fresh long thin red chillies,
    thinly sliced
6 anchovy fillets, roughly chopped
250 ml dry white wine
1 × 600 g piece tuna, cut into
    2 cm pieces (taken from
    the top-quarter)
finely grated zest and juice
    of 1 lemon
2 handfuls rocket
sea salt flakes and freshly
    ground white pepper
1 quantity Pangrattato
    (see page 188)

Pumpkin, Caramelised Onion and Goat's Curd Pizza

1 Preheat a fan-forced oven to 180°C.

2 Place the pumpkin on a non-stick baking tray. Drizzle with 1 tablespoon of the olive and sprinkle with salt. Roast for 25 minutes or until tender, turning occasionally. Set aside.

3 Place the onion and 1 tablespoon of the olive oil in a 24 cm heavy-based non-stick frying pan, then cook over medium heat, stirring occasionally, for 30 minutes or until it deepens in colour and softens. Add the vinegar and stir. Remove from the heat and set aside.

4 Place a pizza stone in the oven. Preheat the oven to 220°C–240°C.

5 Roll out a thin disc of dough to form a 26 cm round and brush with olive oil, leaving a 1 cm border. Sprinkle the base with provolone, leaving a 1 cm border, then top with the pumpkin, caramelised onion and thyme. Place the pizza onto the stone and bake for 4–5 minutes or until the pizza crust is bubbly and golden. Remove from the oven, brush the edge with a little olive oil and scatter dollops of goat's curd over the top. Scatter with spinach, then season with a little salt and pepper. Serve immediately.

Makes 1

¼ small jap pumpkin, peeled, seeded, cut into 2 cm chunks
100 ml olive oil
sea salt flakes
1 onion, thinly sliced
1 tablespoon sherry vinegar
¼ quantity pizza dough (see page 70)
75 g provolone cheese, grated
2 sprigs thyme
75 g goat's curd
1 small handful of baby spinach, washed, trimmed
freshly ground black pepper

Bolognese and Sopressa Salami Pizza

A good bolognese sauce such as the Oxtail Bolognese on page 65 is essential for this recipe, so the next time you make spag bol pop a little of the sauce into a ziplock bag or plastic container and put it in the freezer for your next pizza day.

1 Place a pizza stone in a fan-forced oven. Preheat the oven to 220–240°C.

2 Roll out a thin disc of dough to form a 26 cm round and brush with olive oil, leaving a 1 cm border. Spread the bolognese over the pizza base, leaving a 1 cm border, then sprinkle with the mozzarella. Place the salami slices over the base, overlapping each other. Sprinkle with oregano.

3 Place the pizza onto the stone and bake for 4–5 minutes or until the pizza crust is bubbly and golden. Serve immediately.

Makes 1

¼ quantity Pizza Dough (see page 70)
1 tablespoon extra virgin olive oil
150 g Oxtail Bolognese (see page 65)
80 g mozzarella, grated
12 thin slices sopressa salami
1 tablespoon oregano leaves

Calamari, Prawn and Salsa Verde Pizza

Makes 1

1 small calamari
3 raw prawns, peeled and cleaned
sea salt flakes and freshly ground
    white pepper
¼ quantity **Pizza Dough** (see page 70)
olive oil, for brushing
50 g provolone cheese, shredded
50 g mozzarella cheese, shredded
4 thin slices flat pancetta
1 small handful rocket

SALSA VERDE
2 tablespoons chopped
    flat-leaf parsley
1 tablespoon chopped dill
1 tablespoon salted capers,
    rinsed, drained, chopped
1 clove garlic, chopped
finely grated zest of 1 lemon
30 ml extra virgin olive oil
sea salt flakes and freshly
    ground white pepper

Fresh raw prawns and calamari will make an enormous difference to the taste of this pizza, so substitute with frozen ones at your peril!

1 To clean the calamari, rinse and then separate the hood and tentacles. Rinse and remove the contents of the hood and rinse again. Remove the head and beak from the tentacles and rinse again. Remove the quill from the hood and discard, then thinly slice the hood.

2 Cut the prawns lengthways in half and half again lengthways. Drizzle the prawns and calamari with a little olive oil and season with salt and pepper.

3 For the salsa verde, combine the parsley, dill, capers, garlic, lemon zest and olive oil in a small bowl, then season with salt and pepper, stir and set aside.

4 Place a pizza stone in a fan-forced oven. Preheat the oven to 220–240°C.

5 Roll out a thin disc of dough to form a 26 cm round and brush with olive oil, leaving a 1 cm border.

6 Sprinkle the pizza base with the provolone and mozzarella, brush the edge of the pizza base with olive oil and place on top of the pizza stone, then cook for 2–3 minutes or until the pizza puffs up and is slightly golden.

7 Remove the pizza from the oven and randomly scatter the calamari, prawns and pancetta over the top. Return the pizza to the oven for another 3 minutes or until the prawns and calamari are just cooked. Remove from the oven and spoon the salsa verde over the top, then scatter with rocket. Serve immediately.

Pancetta and Potato Pizza

Makes 1

2 small kipfler potatoes, scrubbed
table salt
¼ quantity **Pizza Dough** (see page 70)
3 teaspoons olive oil
75 g provolone cheese, grated
2 stalks rosemary, sprigs picked
sea salt flakes
75 g tallegio cheese, sliced
4 thin slices flat pancetta
1 small handful wild rocket
freshly ground black pepper

1 Place a pizza stone in a fan-forced oven. Preheat the oven to 220–240°C. Meanwhile, cook the potatoes in a small saucepan of simmering salted water over medium heat for 15 minutes or until tender. Drain, then leave until cool enough to handle. Peel and slice widthways into thick rounds.

2 Roll out a thin disc of dough to form a 26 cm round and brush with olive oil, leaving a 1 cm border. Sprinkle the base with provolone and top with potato. Add a sprinkle of rosemary and sea salt. Place the pizza onto the stone and bake for 3 minutes. Remove from the oven and scatter the tallegio and pancetta randomly over the pizza, then return to the oven for another 2 minutes or until the pizza crust is crisp and golden. Remove from the oven, brush the sides with a little olive oil and scatter with wild rocket, then season with pepper. Serve immediately.

Beetroot Risotto with Persian Feta and Baby Basil

Serves 4

2 medium-sized beetroot, washed
150 g rock salt
500 ml Chicken Stock (see page 183)
60 g unsalted butter, chopped
½ onion, finely chopped
1 clove garlic, finely chopped
1 teaspoon table salt
200 g carnaroli rice
100 ml dry white wine
freshly ground white pepper
120 g Persian feta
extra virgin olive oil and baby basil
    (optional), to serve

Notes

- *For perfect risotto, buy good-quality risotto rice. My first choice is carnaroli, a nice elliptical grain that creates a lovely viscous risotto while maintaining its shape as it absorbs the stock.*

- *The finished risotto should be fluid and loose and the grains be al dente (have a little firm bite) and bound together by a thick, luscious sauce.*

Risotto should be soft and luscious, never thick and stodgy. Most risotto recipes tell you to add a little of the hot stock at a time and stir. I prefer to add all the boiling stock in one go and only stir it at the end of cooking. I find that this still releases the starch from the rice but keeps the grains intact. The rice should be a touch al dente but never chalky; it is a fine line but once you achieve it your risotto will soar.

1   Preheat a fan-forced oven to 160°C. Place the beetroot on a bed of rock salt on a baking tray. Roast for 40 minutes or until tender. Peel and cut one-third of the beetroot into 1 cm dice. Puree the remaining beetroot in a food processor until smooth (you should have 250 ml puree). Set aside.

2   Bring the stock to the boil in a small saucepan over high heat. Melt 30 g of the butter in a low wide-based saucepan or non-stick frying pan over medium heat and cook the onion and garlic for 2–3 minutes or until translucent, then add the salt. Add the rice and cook over low heat for a further 2–3 minutes. Add the wine, then allow to reduce, stirring. Add the boiling stock all at once and bring to a simmer; avoid stirring. The stock should be absorbed gradually; it usually takes 15 minutes.

3   After 15 minutes, as the risotto stiffens and absorbs the stock but is still loose, stir in the beetroot puree and cook for a further 2 minutes over low heat. Add the remaining butter and stir in to enrich, then season to taste with salt and pepper.

4   Spoon the risotto onto 4 plates, tapping each one to flatten it a little. Crumble over the feta and sprinkle with a few pieces of beetroot, then dress with a little olive oil. Sprinkle over baby basil leaves (if using) and serve.

Cauliflower Risotto with Calamari and Hazelnuts

Cauliflower is now one of my favourite vegetables, especially when roasted and pureed. As a kid I could never have imagined the humble cauli could be so good. There are lots of elements to this dish so if you decide to drop one or two I won't be upset! But promise to have a go at the risotto itself – you won't be disappointed. Instead of using the calamari you could drizzle over a little lemony browned butter, either with or without the hazelnuts.

1   Bring the stock to the boil in a large saucepan over high heat. Using a low wide-based non-stick frying pan, melt 30 g of the butter over medium heat and cook the onion and garlic for 2–3 minutes or until translucent, then add a pinch of salt. Add the rice and cook over low heat for a further 2–3 minutes. Add the wine, then reduce and stir. Add the boiling stock all at once and bring to a simmer; avoid stirring. The stock should be absorbed gradually; it usually takes 15 minutes.

2   Meanwhile, bring the shredded cauliflower, milk and a pinch of salt to the boil in a saucepan. Reduce the heat to low and simmer for 8–10 minutes or until tender. Drain and reserve the milk. Blend the cauliflower in a blender or using a stick blender until a smooth and creamy puree forms, adding a little of the reserved milk if required. Set aside.

3   Place the cauliflower florets, olive oil and remaining butter in a saucepan, then cook over medium heat for 8–10 minutes or until golden. Remove the cauliflower from the pan and set aside, reserving the butter/oil mixture.

4   To clean the calamari, rinse and then separate the hood and tentacles. Rinse and remove the contents of the hood and rinse again. Remove the head and beak from the tentacles and rinse. Remove the quill from the hood, then cut the hoods into 4 cm pieces.

5   Heat a little of the reserved butter/oil mixture in the saucepan or a large non-stick frying pan over high heat, then quickly sear the calamari. As the calamari begins to colour, add the cauliflower florets and hazelnuts. Season with a pinch of salt and the lemon juice, then remove from the heat.

6   Gently stir the cauliflower puree into the rice and cook for another 2 minutes; the rice should have absorbed all the stock and be slightly al dente.

7   Divide the risotto between 4 plates, tapping each one to flatten it a little. Spoon the calamari/cauliflower mixture over the risotto and drizzle with a little of the butter mixture from the cooking, then serve immediately.

Serves 4

500 ml Chicken Stock (see page 183)
150 g unsalted butter, chopped
½ onion, finely chopped
1 clove garlic, finely chopped
table salt
200 g carnaroli rice
100 ml dry white wine
1 small cauliflower, ¼ cut into small florets and the remainder finely shredded
400 ml milk
1 tablespoon olive oil
800 g–1 kg calamari (to yield 720 g cleaned calamari)
65 g hazelnuts, peeled
squeeze of lemon juice

Notes

- *When it comes to buying risotto rice, carnaroli is my favourite but arborio is fine too. Find a good-quality rice – although it may cost more, it forms the bulk of the meal so it is still cheap in comparison (80–100 g raw rice per person is plenty).*

- *To peel the hazelnuts, roast them on a baking tray at 180℃ for 6 minutes or until the skins loosen. Wrap the hot hazelnuts in a clean tea towel and rub together to peel.*

- *Mum would never clean seafood in the house because of its smell. It made me laugh but now my wife is the same – come on girls! Fresh seafood should smell of the sea. When cleaning calamari work at the sink. The results are worth the effort and much better than using prepared calamari hoods.*

Poultry and Meat

Roast Chicken with Fondant Potato and Minted Peas and Spinach

Buy a good-quality, corn-fed, free-range chicken, remove the wishbone to make it easier to carve and truss it to help hold its form for best results. The flavour of the pan juices is far superior to those from an everyday chicken.

1 Preheat a fan-forced oven to 180°C.

2 To remove the wishbone from the chicken, lift the neck skin to reveal the breast. Scrape the point of a small sharp knife down the wishbone (it looks like an upside-down 'V' shape). Put your fingers behind the bone and tug to remove it. Stuff the cavity with the lemon, thyme and 1 clove of the garlic. Truss the chicken with kitchen twine to hold its form.

3 Heat a flameproof roasting pan over high heat. Season the chicken with salt and pour the olive oil into the pan. Brown the chicken lightly on all sides, starting with one leg, turning it over to brown the other leg, then the breast. Turn the chicken onto its back, then roast for 20 minutes.

4 Baste the chicken with the pan juices. Add the shallots and remaining garlic and roast for a further 40 minutes or until the chicken is cooked. To test, pierce the thigh at the thickest part; the juices should run clear. Transfer the chicken to a large plate and rest for 10 minutes.

5 Meanwhile, for the fondant potato, melt the butter in a deep heavy-based frying pan over medium heat. As the butter begins to bubble, add the potato and thyme in layers. Reduce the heat to low, then cook for 10 minutes or until the potato is golden. Turn the potato over and cook for another 10 minutes or until golden. Add the water; the butter will foam and darken slightly. Baste the potato well and continue to cook for another 10 minutes or until tender. To check, insert the point of a sharp knife into the centre of a potato; it should be soft and tender. Remove from the heat, then leave to stand for 5 minutes. Season with salt. Set aside and keep warm.

6 Place the roasting pan of cooking juices over low heat, then crush the roasted garlic and shallots into the pan with the back of a fork. Add the wine and stock and simmer over low heat for 2 minutes. Set aside.

7 For the minted peas and spinach, warm the olive oil in a saucepan over low heat, then add the garlic and leave to infuse for 30 seconds. Add the peas and increase the heat to medium, then cook for 2 minutes or until they are warmed through. Add the spinach and mint, then remove from the heat and stir, allowing the spinach to wilt.

8 Cut the chicken into quarters and serve with the fondant potato, gravy and minted peas and spinach.

Serves 4

1 × 1.6 kg free-range chicken
1 lemon, quartered
2 sprigs thyme
2 cloves garlic, peeled
kitchen twine
table salt
30 ml olive oil
5 small shallots, peeled
splash of dry white wine
100 ml Chicken Stock (see page 183)

FONDANT POTATO
170 g unsalted butter, chopped
4 large desiree potatoes,
    cut into 7 cm × 5 cm × 1 cm-
    thick rectangles
4 sprigs thyme
100 ml water
sea salt flakes

MINTED PEAS AND SPINACH
125 ml olive oil
1 small clove garlic, thinly sliced
240 g fresh or frozen peas, washed
2 handfuls spinach, washed
16 mint leaves, washed and chopped

Notes

- *Know thy chicken! Buying a good-quality chicken means one that is fresh not frozen, corn or grain-fed and free-range. Small steps in the right direction reward you handsomely at the table.*

- *I owned a flimsy, hand-me-down roasting pan that Mum gave me when I left home. It travelled with me to Australia. Then I bought a heavy-duty non-stick Scanpan roasting pan eight years ago – it was an epiphany and roasting has been a pleasure ever since.*

Coq au Vin

Serves 4

1 × 1.4 kg free-range chicken,
    cut into 8 pieces (see Notes)
400 ml red wine
150 ml ruby port
2 cloves garlic, peeled
20 shallots, peeled
1 × 300 g piece bacon, rind
    removed and discarded,
    cut into 1.5 cm pieces
3 sprigs thyme
1 fresh bay leaf
2 tablespoons olive oil
16 button mushrooms,
    stalks trimmed
table salt and freshly ground
    white pepper
200 ml Veal Stock (see page 182)
400 ml Chicken Stock (see page 183)
1½ tablespoons cornflour
1 teaspoon water
crusty bread or Home-style Mash,
    to serve (see page 188)

Notes

- *You can substitute chicken maryland pieces but I recommend using a whole chicken as it is more economical.*

- *It takes a little practice to divide a whole chicken into pieces. First remove the legs, then separate the drumsticks and thighs. Remove the backbone and set aside, then divide the breasts. Cut each breast into 2 pieces on the bone. Cut the carcass into pieces and reserve for making stock (see page 183).*

- *The marinade is brought to the boil in a separate pan in order to skim and strain away any coagulated juices (blood), resulting in a finer, shiny sauce.*

Coq au vin is an all-time classic, you can't beat it – not only is it rich and warming but it is packed with flavour. There is no way around it, you need more than a good slosh of red wine to make this dish something really special. If you feel that's too extravagant, then by all means be a little more frugal with the wine and port; I'll leave it up to you. You will need to marinate the chicken the day before you wish to serve it.

1   Place the chicken, wine and port in a large non-reactive dish, then add the garlic, shallots, bacon, thyme and bay leaf. Cover and refrigerate for 24 hours.

2   Drain the chicken, garlic, shallots and bacon well, reserving the marinade. Pat the chicken dry with paper towel if necessary.

3   Heat the oil in a flameproof casserole or large heavy-based saucepan over high heat, then add the bacon from the marinade and cook until a light-golden brown. Remove and set aside. Cook the shallots from the marinade for 2–3 minutes or until a light-golden brown, then remove and set aside. Add the mushrooms to the pan and cook for 2–3 minutes, then remove and set aside.

4   Season the chicken with salt and pepper, then add to the pan and brown over medium heat on all sides for 4–5 minutes. Meanwhile, bring the marinade to the boil in a saucepan over high heat. Skim the surface, then strain through a fine strainer, reserving the thyme and bay leaf.

5   Return the shallots and bacon to the pan of chicken and immediately pour in the hot marinade. Return to the boil over high heat and simmer for 4–5 minutes or until the liquid has reduced by two-thirds. Add both stocks and the reserved garlic, thyme and bay leaf. Bring back to the boil and turn the heat down to low, then simmer, covered, for a further 45 minutes.

6   Remove the chicken, bacon, mushrooms and shallots from the pan and set aside. Strain the sauce through a fine strainer, reserving the bay leaf. Return the sauce to the pan and bring it back to the boil over high heat. Mix the cornflour with the water, then whisk it into the sauce. Reduce the heat to low and simmer for 5 minutes or until the sauce thickens.

7   Return the chicken, bacon, mushrooms, shallots and bay leaf to the pan and simmer for a further 5 minutes or until warmed through. Serve with crusty bread or mashed potato.

Vietnamese Chicken Coleslaw

Once tried, this Vietnamese-inspired coleslaw will become a firm favourite – it's so fresh and very more-ish. Trips to your local Asian grocer will reveal so many new ingredients, such as little packets of crispy garlic and shallots, different crackers and garlic chives. Buy and try – that's my motto!

1   Place the chicken in a large saucepan and cover with cold water. Add the coriander roots, garlic, chilli and lemongrass. Bring to the boil over high heat, then reduce the heat to medium and cook for 30 minutes. Turn off the heat and leave the chicken to cook completely as it cools in the stock.

2   When the chicken is cool enough to handle, remove it from the pan. Strain the stock, then transfer it to an airtight container, label and store in the fridge for up to 5 days or freezer for up to 2 months for making soup. Shred the chicken meat and discard the bones, then place it in a large bowl and set aside.

3   For the nuoc mam dressing, place the palm sugar and 50 ml of the water in a small saucepan over medium heat, stirring to dissolve the sugar; don't let it come to the boil if possible. Set aside to cool. Blend the ginger, garlic, chilli, fish sauce and remaining water in a food processor, then stir it into the cool palm sugar syrup. Add the lime juice and set aside.

4   Add the cabbage, carrot, onion and mango or pawpaw, coriander leaves, Vietnamese mint and bean sprouts to the chicken and mix through. Spoon over a generous amount of the dressing (keep leftover dressing in an airtight container in the fridge for up to 10 days and serve with grilled fish or chicken). Add the crispy shallots, sesame seeds and fried garlic.

5   Spoon the salad into bowls, then scatter with a little more coriander and Vietnamese mint and throw on some sesame crackers, then serve.

Notes

- Poaching is such a lovely way to cook chicken. The bonus is that you get free chicken stock at the end with no extra effort. Because poaching is done at such a low temperature (around 100℃) shrinkage is minimal and the resulting meat is moist and tender.

- As the chicken cools in the stock it cooks completely without using further heat. The chicken effectively 'rests' in the stock as it cools, resulting in tender, juicy meat.

- Dissolving the palm sugar in only a portion of the dressing gives it an element of freshness, which is in keeping with the overall fresh flavours of the salad.

Serves 4

1 × 1 kg free-range chicken
½ cup coriander leaves, well washed and stalks and roots reserved
2 cloves garlic, peeled
1 fresh long thin red chilli, split
1 stick lemongrass, white part only, bruised with the back of a knife
½ small Chinese cabbage, finely shredded
1 carrot, finely shredded
½ red onion, thinly sliced
1 green mango or green pawpaw, finely shredded
¼ cup Vietnamese mint leaves, plus extra to serve
2 large handfuls of bean sprouts
½ cup crispy shallots (see page 195)
3 tablespoons sesame seeds
3 tablespoons fried garlic (see page 196)
sesame crackers (see page 197) and coriander leaves, to serve

NUOC MAM DRESSING
75 g grated palm sugar
100 ml water
small piece of ginger, chopped
1 clove garlic, peeled
1 fresh long thin red chilli
100 ml fish sauce
juice of 2 limes

Chicken, Bacon and Mushroom Pies

Nothing says comfort food more than a pie, be it apple, steak and mushroom or, in this case, a luscious chicken pie. It is rare to find someone who doesn't like a pie. The sad thing is that most of us only know commercially made versions with a nondescript filling and lacklustre pastry. Now I'm not saying that I never get the urge to eat a pie and sauce on the run, but there's nothing like a chunky homemade pie filled with tender pieces of meat and vegetables, all encased in a crisp golden crust of gorgeous pastry. Go on, give it a go!

1 Bring the milk, bay leaves and a pinch of salt and pepper to the boil in a saucepan over high heat. Remove from the heat and remove the bay leaves, reserving 1 and discarding the remainder. Meanwhile, melt 50 g of the butter in another saucepan over medium heat. Add the flour to the butter and stir to combine, then cook, stirring regularly, for 3 minutes (this mixture is known as a roux). Pour one-quarter of the hot milk into the roux and stir over medium heat until smooth. Add another quarter of the milk and repeat until all the milk has been incorporated into the sauce. Bring to a gentle simmer and cook over low heat for a further 5 minutes, stirring regularly to prevent the mixture from sticking.

2 Melt the remaining butter in a large saucepan over low heat. Add the chicken, mushrooms, onions, bacon, thyme, garlic and reserved bay leaf and cook over low heat for 3–4 minutes or until the chicken whitens and the bacon releases a little fat. Add the wine and a little more salt and pepper. Increase the heat to medium and simmer for 4 minutes or until the wine has reduced by half. Add the white sauce to the chicken and bring to a slow simmer. Cook covered over low heat for 20 minutes, stirring occasionally.

3 Meanwhile, for the pastry, mix the flour, suet mix and a pinch of salt in a large bowl. Make a well in the centre, then pour in the water and gently mix by hand until it just comes together to form a ball; add extra flour if necessary. Turn the dough ball onto a floured surface. Roll out until 3 mm–thick, then cut into 6 squares, 1 cm bigger all around than the pie moulds or dishes (my moulds are 5 cm wide × 4 cm deep). Leave to rest in the fridge for 30 minutes.

4 Preheat a fan-forced oven to 165°C.

5 Divide the chicken mixture between the pie moulds. Wet the lip of the moulds with water and top each one with a piece of pastry. Tuck the pastry down a little around the edges. Brush with the beaten egg and make a small incision with the tip of a knife in the centre of each pastry lid to allow steam to escape. Rest in the fridge for 10 minutes. Repeat this process twice (this helps create a super-golden crust). Place the pie moulds on a baking tray to catch any sauce. Bake the pies for 30 minutes or until golden, then serve.

Serves 6

700 ml milk
4 fresh bay leaves
table salt and freshly ground white pepper
75 g unsalted butter, chopped
75 g plain flour
1 × 1.4 kg free-range chicken, cut into 8 pieces (see Notes page 83), then boned or 900 g chicken breast or thigh fillets, cut into bite-sized pieces
250 g button mushrooms, stalks trimmed
12 baby onions, peeled
1 × 250 g piece bacon, rind removed and discarded, cut into 2 cm chunks
2 sprigs thyme
2 cloves garlic, thinly sliced
80 ml dry white wine

SUET PASTRY
150 g self-raising flour, plus extra if needed and for dusting
150 g suet mix (see page 197)
table salt
180 ml chilled water
1 free-range egg yolk, beaten with a pinch of salt

Notes

- *I use a piece of bacon here rather than pre-sliced rashers. I can cut it into nice, meaty chunks, which adds both flavour and texture. Bacon pieces can be purchased in larger supermarkets.*

- *Always allow pastry to rest after rolling and cutting it, as well as before baking once it has been placed on the pie. This prevents it from shrinking.*

Duck Confit with Warm Brussels Sprout and Bacon Salad

By rights, duck confit is one of those preparations that have no place in the modern world. Its origins come from those living on the land – a peasant dish devised to cook the toughest goose or duck, then preserve it in its own fat to see you through the long, hard winter months. I remember doing a work placement (known as a 'stage') in a famous London restaurant and, after working fourteen hours one day, sitting down to a confit of goose necks and legs for the evening meal around a crowded kitchen bench. A hardworking farmer I am not, but it tasted delicious! The duck needs to be coated in a spiced salt mixture and refrigerated for twelve to twenty-four hours before you start cooking. However, the crisp skin of a well-cooked duck confit and the soft meat that falls apart under the pressure of an eagerly held fork is worth this time and effort. If you wish to confit the duck in advance, it can be stored in the fridge covered in the reserved fat for up to two weeks.

1 Crush the peppercorns, clove and star anise with a mortar and pestle, then mix with the rock salt. Sprinkle half of the salt mixture into a 2 litre-capacity ceramic dish. Place the duck marylands on the salt and sprinkle over the remaining salt mixture. Cover with plastic film and refrigerate for 12–24 hours.

2 Preheat a fan-forced oven to 140°C.

3 Brush off and discard the salt mixture from the duck, then pat it dry with paper towel. Lay the duck, skin-side down, in a baking dish or roasting pan and place in the oven. The fat will begin to render after 15 minutes. Top up the pan with the rendered duck fat until the duck is just covered, then add the thyme and bay leaves. Continue to cook for another 1 hour or until the duck is tender. Remove the duck and strain the fat. Leave the fat to cool, then set aside. Reduce the oven temperature to 100°C, then return the duck to the pan and put into the oven while you prepare the sprouts.

4 For the salad, pour 30 ml of the reserved duck fat into a heavy-based non-stick frying pan. Add the butter and melt over medium heat. When the butter begins to bubble, fry the bacon and garlic for 3 minutes or until golden. Add the sprouts and cook for another 3–4 minutes, keeping the sprouts firm to the bite. Add the vinegar and cook for another 1 minute. Remove from the heat, then season with salt and add a few turns of pepper.

5 Serve the duck with the warm brussels sprout and bacon salad.

Serves 4

6 white peppercorns
1 clove
½ star anise
2 tablespoons rock salt
4 duck marylands
300 ml rendered duck fat
  (see page 195)
2 sprigs thyme
2 fresh bay leaves

WARM BRUSSELS SPROUT AND
  BACON SALAD
30 g unsalted butter
4 rashers bacon, rind removed,
  thinly sliced
2 cloves garlic, thinly sliced
16 brussels sprouts, finely sliced
  (see Notes)
60 ml red-wine vinegar
table salt and freshly ground
  white pepper

Notes

• *If you prefer crisp-skin duck (see opposite), then place the duck, skin-side down, in a frying pan with 1 teaspoon duck fat before cooking the brussels sprout salad. Crisp it up over medium heat, basting regularly with the fat in the pan, for 2–3 minutes. Remove and keep warm while you cook the sprouts.*

• *I use a mandoline to slice the sprouts. It is a worthwhile purchase as it allows you to achieve a very fine cut without practising those knife skills. I like the green, Japanese plastic-based ones sold in Asian food stores. They are inexpensive but very sharp, so watch those fingers!*

Braised Rabbit with Borlotti Beans, Globe Artichokes and Lemon

Serves 4

2 tablespoons extra virgin olive oil, plus extra for drizzling
1 × 2 kg rabbit, cut into 8 pieces
table salt
1 tablespoon plain flour
4 cloves garlic, peeled
1 onion, sliced
200 ml dry white wine
1.2 litres Chicken Stock (see page 183)
4 sprigs thyme
4 fresh bay leaves
650 g fresh borlotti bean pods, podded (to yield 200 g beans)
4 globe artichokes
1 lemon, halved, plus finely grated zest and juice of 1 lemon
freshly ground white pepper
2 tablespoons flat-leaf parsley leaves
crusty bread, to serve

Notes

- *You can also use dried borlotti beans. Soak 400 g beans in cold water the night before you wish to cook this recipe, then follow the instructions on page 194.*

- *Rabbit is very versatile, however it is extremely lean so you have to be careful not to overcook it or it will become dry and unpalatable. I use rabbit legs a lot in my cooking because they are meaty and tender and take on other flavours, whether marinated, wrapped or stuffed, beautifully.*

You will need to ask your butcher for a plump farmed rabbit – they are not widely available because restaurants tend to grab all the available stock. Farmed rabbit is more tender than wild rabbit, not to mention plumper and bigger. Its flesh also tends to be paler, almost milky white, and its flavour is mild – similar to that of chicken. A rabbit can be broken down into pieces much like you would tackle a chicken. If you ask nicely, your butcher might do this for you. Alternatively, use a good-quality grain-fed 1.6 kilogram chicken. Try to use fresh borlotti beans when they are in season during springtime as they are fantastic.

1   Heat the olive oil in a non-stick saute pan, heavy-based saucepan or flameproof casserole over high heat. Season the rabbit with salt and dust with flour. Fry the rabbit for 3–4 minutes or until golden. Add the garlic and onion and cook for 1 minute, then add the wine and cook for a further 3–4 minutes or until reduced by half. Add the stock, thyme, bay leaves and borlotti beans. Once the mixture boils, reduce the heat to low and simmer, covered, for 20 minutes.

2   Meanwhile, prepare the artichokes, working one at a time. Strip down the outer leaves until you reveal the heart at the base. Peel the stem and base with a vegetable peeler to remove the outer green layer. Rub the artichoke quickly with the cut lemon or it will turn brown. Chop the top off about halfway down the bulb of each artichoke. Use a dessertspoon to scoop out the fibrous matter (choke) from inside the artichoke heart. Cut each artichoke in half lengthways, then rub with lemon again. Immediately add the artichokes to the pan. Cover and cook for another 20 minutes or until the rabbit, beans and artichokes are tender.

3   Remove and discard the thyme, then add a few grinds of pepper, a drizzle of olive oil and the parsley. Stir in the lemon zest and juice, then serve with crusty bread.

Braised Lamb Neck with Fennel and Olives

This dish is inspired by Angelo Sanfilippo, my chef at The Boathouse. His parents come from Foggia in the southwest of Italy, where lamb and fennel cooked with olives make a regular appearance on the family's table. Whether they would be happy with my rendition remains to be seen. This works really well accompanied by either some crusty bread, a nice dish of potatoes crushed with extra virgin olive oil or crisp-fried or wet polenta.

1 Preheat a fan-forced oven to 120°C.

2 Heat a heavy-based ovenproof saucepan or enamelled cast-iron casserole over high heat and add the olive oil. Season the lamb with salt and pepper and brown well for 5–6 minutes. Remove the lamb and set aside.

3 Add the fennel, onion and garlic to the pan and cook over high heat for 8 minutes or until golden. Add the thyme, bay leaf and wine and simmer until the wine has almost evaporated. Add the veal stock and return the lamb to the pan, then bring to the boil. Skim off any fat that has floated to the top. Cover and cook in the oven for 3 hours or until tender.

4 Remove the lamb from the pan and set aside. Reduce the sauce over high heat by half to intensify its flavour; there should be just enough sauce left to serve 4. Return the lamb to the pan and add the olives to warm through.

5 Divide the lamb between 4 plates, then season to taste and spoon the sauce over the lamb. Drizzle with olive oil, garnish with rosemary sprigs (if using), and serve with crusty bread, if desired.

Serves 4

30 ml olive oil, plus extra
    for drizzling
4 lamb neck fillets
table salt and freshly ground
    white pepper
1 bulb fennel, sliced
1 onion, sliced
2 cloves garlic, sliced
1 sprig thyme
½ fresh bay leaf
100 ml white wine
800 ml Veal Stock (see page 182)
100 g kalamata olives, pitted
rosemary sprigs with flowers
    intact (optional) and crusty
    bread, to serve

Notes

- *If you can, buy your braising meat whole – a good butcher will always dispense advice and it won't be any more expensive. Either leave whole, as I've done here, or cut into large chunks and brown well; the stew will look and taste so much better for it – rich with big succulent chunks of meat to get your fork into.*

- *A good-quality stock is important if you love flavour-packed stews. The milder the stock, the lighter the stew. To make a strong veal stock, follow the recipe on page 182. This will give the finished sauce a deeper flavour.*

Vitello Tonnato

Serves 4

1 × 450 g veal scotch fillet
kitchen twine
1.5 litres Chicken Stock
    (see page 183) **or water**
125 ml Basic Mayonnaise
    (see page 181)
6 anchovy fillets
3 tablespoons large salted capers,
    rinsed and drained
130 g tinned tuna in oil, drained
finely grated zest and juice of
    ½ lemon
table salt and freshly ground
    white pepper
30 ml extra virgin olive oil
1 lemon, very thinly sliced

Vitello tonnato is a classic Italian dish of cold veal – sounds awful, doesn't it? Believe me, it's not. Made well, it's a great summer dish and my first choice if I spy it on a menu. It has to be good though, which means perfectly pink, well-seasoned veal and a smooth, delicate tuna sauce with a hint of anchovy and a kick of lemon and salty capers. The secret is not to smother the veal with too much sauce. Rather, make it look pretty, with generous but restrained (yes it is possible) dollops of tuna sauce and a light drizzle of grassy extra virgin olive oil, finished with wafer-thin slices of lemon that you can eat but not squeeze. Bring me summer and a table in the sun!

1   Tie the veal neatly with twine to hold its shape. Place the veal in a saucepan and cover with chicken stock or water. Bring to the boil over high heat, then reduce the heat to low and simmer for 35 minutes. To test if the veal is ready, insert a meat thermometer into the centre – it should register 48°C for medium–done. Alternatively, insert a metal skewer then place it on your bottom lip; it should be just warm in the centre. Transfer the veal to a plate and leave to cool for 1 hour. When cool, slice thinly and set aside.

2   Blend the mayonnaise, 2 of the anchovies, 2 tablespoons of the capers, tuna, lemon zest and juice in a food processor until creamy and smooth. Season with a pinch of salt and a few twists of pepper.

3   Spoon a little of the sauce onto a large plate and spread out. Place the veal slices on top and spoon over a little more of the sauce. Drizzle with olive oil and scatter with the remaining capers, anchovies and the very thin lemon slices, then serve.

Notes

· *Veal is a beautiful meat, but you have to trust your butcher here as what is often sold labelled as veal isn't. I like to use the scotch fillet and rib loin of veal. As veal comes from a young animal it doesn't have a lot of fat, so overcooking can result in dry meat.*

· *Tying the veal with kitchen twine means that it holds its shape during cooking. It is also easier to carve evenly, which improves its presentation.*

· *Soaking the salted capers in a good quantity of water will help soften their saltiness. For best results, lift the capers from the water, leaving the salt granules behind.*

Veal Saltimbocca

Veal saltimbocca is an Italian classic that matches veal with cured pork and sage. Over time it has crossed the boundaries from veal to chicken and fish – the combination of bacon and sage travels well! Normally this dish is cooked quickly using the best cuts of veal, which come from the loin and backstrap. However, this is expensive. The tougher – and cheaper – cuts can be used instead and then braised until tender. Italian friends of mine make a braised version that I love and, to be honest, prefer, so I've included it here. The flavour is terrific and it makes a super winter dish but is light enough to serve in summer with a crisp salad such as the Shredded Cabbage and Fennel Salad with Parmesan on page 53. Veal can be bought as bobby, which is a very young male calf that is light and milky in colour. Older calves, which have had a chance to nibble on grass, are bigger and have darker, pinker meat – I think this has more flavour.

1   Preheat a fan-forced oven to 165°C.

2   Heat a saucepan over medium heat, then add 30 ml of the olive oil. Cook the onion and garlic for 2 minutes to soften the onion and release the flavour from the garlic. Add the thyme, bay leaves and tomato paste, then stir and cook for a further 2 minutes. Add the tomato and water, then bring to a gentle simmer. Remove from the heat and set aside.

3   Lay a slice of prosciutto on the bench and place 2 sage leaves across the centre. Lay a veal slice on top and fold the prosciutto over the veal, then turn over and set aside. Repeat with the remaining prosciutto, sage and veal.

4   Heat a heavy-based non-stick frying pan over high heat and pour in the remaining olive oil. Working in batches, fry the veal quickly on each side until golden. Remove the veal and place it in an ovenproof frying pan or roasting pan large enough to hold the veal slices in one slightly overlapping layer. Cover with the tomato sauce, then add the remaining sage and seal with a lid or sheet of foil.

5   Bake the veal for 45–60 minutes or until tender. Season the veal saltimbocca with salt and pepper, then serve with the cabbage and fennel salad to the side, if desired.

Serves 4

80 ml olive oil
½ onion, finely chopped
2 cloves garlic, finely chopped
1 sprig thyme, leaves picked
2 fresh bay leaves
2 tablespoons tomato paste
2 × 400 g tins chopped tomato
100 ml water
8 slices prosciutto
24 sage leaves
1 × 640 g veal loin, scotch fillet or topside, cut into 8 × 80 g slices
sea salt flakes and freshly ground black pepper
Shredded Fennel and Cabbage Salad with Parmesan (optional, see page 53), **to serve**

Notes

- *Tougher cuts of veal include silverside, girello (nut of veal) and topside. Butchers often tenderise veal by passing it through a machine that effectively mashes it, which they sell labelled as schnitzel. This damages the meat, which in turn dries out during cooking – not ideal unless you like eating cardboard.*

- *The tender prime or sweet veal cuts such as tenderloin, loin and scotch, or what can be sold as 'cube roll' or backstrap, are more expensive. However, they are ideal for quickly pan-frying and then serving immediately.*

- *It is preferable to pan-fry the veal in batches so that the pan is not overcrowded as this ensures that the temperature is maintained so the meat seals rather than stews.*

Crumbed Pork with Roasted Quince and Hazelnuts

Quinces are such a beautiful autumn fruit and, although they have become more popular in recent years, they are still not a regular ingredient in most kitchens. Once you get over the fact that they are very hard and have a velvety fuzz on their thick yellow skins you will find that they are surprisingly easy to prepare and readily cross the boundary between savoury and sweet dishes. After roasting them, as I've done here, you will be surprised by the result and hopefully be inspired to use them more often.

1   Preheat a fan-forced oven to 180°C.

2   Roast the hazelnuts on a baking tray for 8 minutes, then transfer to a clean tea towel and rub to remove the skins – don't worry if a little bit of skin remains. Set aside to cool.

3   Squeeze the lemon juice into a bowl of cold water. Peel the quinces quickly with a peeler and cut into quarters. Carefully remove the cores with a paring knife, then place the quince in the lemon water to prevent discoloration.

4   Place an ovenproof heavy-based non-stick frying pan over medium heat and add a dash of the olive oil. Cook the quince for 3–4 minutes, turning over carefully so it colours lightly and evenly. Transfer to the oven and roast for 15 minutes, turning once or twice until tender.

5   Meanwhile, add the milk to the beaten egg. Coat the pork cutlets with flour, patting off the excess, then coat with the beaten egg mixture and then the breadcrumbs. Pat the cutlets to ensure the breadcrumbs have adhered to the pork.

6   Heat the remaining olive oil in a large heavy-based non-stick frying pan over low heat and pan-fry the cutlets for 6–8 minutes on each side or until golden and crisp.

7   Remove the quince from the oven and place the pan over medium heat, then toss in the hazelnuts and butter. Baste the quince well with the butter and season with a little salt and pepper. Add the verjuice to the pan and reduce until it has almost evaporated. Remove from the heat.

8   Place a pork cutlet on each plate, then place 4 quince pieces neatly around it, sprinkle a few hazelnuts over the quince and drizzle with the pan juices. Sprinkle with baby basil (if using) or watercress and serve with lemon wedges to the side.

Serves 4

2 tablespoons hazelnuts
juice of ½ lemon
4 quinces
50 ml olive oil
30 ml milk
1 free-range egg, beaten
4 pork cutlets, French-trimmed (optional, ask your butcher to do this)
2 tablespoons plain flour
100 g fresh breadcrumbs
20 g unsalted butter
table salt and freshly ground black pepper
2 tablespoons verjuice (see page 197)
baby basil leaves (optional) or watercress sprig and lemon wedges, to serve

Notes

· *The secret to cooking a good crumbed cutlet is patience. If you start cooking it slowly over low heat and resist the temptation to turn it over before it's time, the crust will brown beautifully.*

· *If you are feeling extravagant then add a couple of teaspoons of butter to the pan in the final minutes of cooking the cutlets. Leave it to bubble and brown around the cutlets, then taste the pan juices and season. Remove the cutlets from the pan and drizzle with the pan juices.*

Roasted Pork Belly with Garlic and Braised Red Cabbage

Pork belly used to be cheap – so cheap in fact that no one wanted it. Then we cottoned onto the fact that it not only produces the best crackling ever, but is moist, delicate and irresistible. Supply versus demand means that it isn't cheap anymore and you can probably blame us chefs for that. Cooking the belly slowly with the skin-side down gives such a crisp, glazed skin that it looks like a piece of glass. The addition of a spiced salt mix along with plenty of garlic makes for a mighty fine meal. Try and buy a nice thick pork belly – be selective. It is important to score the skin to allow the fat to render during cooking. The salt in the spice mixture draws the moisture away from the fat, which also helps the cause! A word of warning – take it easy when it comes to tucking in otherwise you'll grow a little pork belly of your own. Listen to the voice of experience!

1   To start preparing the braised red cabbage, place the cabbage, apple, onion, cinnamon stick and star anise in a bowl. Pour in the red wine, then cover with plastic film and leave to marinate overnight in the fridge. Drain well, reserving the wine and spices.

2   Preheat a fan-forced oven to 165°C.

3   Dry-roast the cumin, star anise and fennel seeds in a frying pan over medium heat for 2 minutes or until fragrant, then add the salt. Grind with a mortar and pestle. Rub the spice mixture all over the pork.

4   Pour the oil into a heavy-based roasting pan or ovenproof frying pan. Place the pork skin-side down in the pan, then roast for 1½ hours, basting it regularly with the pan juices.

5   Meanwhile, to cook the cabbage, melt the butter in an ovenproof heavy-based saucepan or flameproof casserole, then add the cabbage mixture and cook over low heat for 3–4 minutes or until the cabbage begins to soften. Create a well in the centre of the cabbage mixture and add the redcurrant jelly, then leave for 2–3 minutes to bubble and darken. Stir to mix the cabbage and redcurrant jelly. Add the reserved wine and spices, then increase the heat to medium and reduce by two-thirds. Season with salt and pepper, then pop on a lid and cook in the oven for 1 hour.

6   Tip the excess fat away from the pan, leaving just enough for basting the meat. Turn the pork over, then add the garlic to the pan and cook for a further 30 minutes. Remove the pork from the oven and leave to rest, skin-side up, for 10 minutes. Leave the skin exposed to crisp up. Carve the pork, then serve it with the braised red cabbage and roasted garlic.

Serves 6

2 tablespoons cumin seeds
3 star anise
2 teaspoons fennel seeds
2 tablespoons table salt
80 ml olive oil
1 × 2 kg pork belly, boned, skin-on and scored
2 heads garlic, cloves separated

BRAISED RED CABBAGE
1 red cabbage, cored and shredded
2 golden delicious apples, cored, thinly sliced
1 red onion, halved lengthways, then thinly sliced widthways
1 cinnamon stick
2 star anise
1 × 750 ml bottle full-bodied red wine
25 g unsalted butter
3 tablespoons redcurrant jelly
table salt and freshly ground white pepper

Notes

- Starting off by cooking the pork skin-side down helps to render the fat and gives you crisp, glassy crackling. When you rest the pork take care not to cover the crackling as the steam from the meat will soften it.

Seafood

Beer-battered Fish with Fat Chips and Tartare Sauce

Fish and chips are the perfect example of how emotive food can be. Great meals are often a sum of the experience. A meal can be presented perfectly, but you still don't enjoy it because something just didn't feel right. We have a saying in the restaurant industry, 'perfect delivery, imperfect experience'. However, fish and chips somehow transcends this. It reminds me of summer holidays by the sea, feasting on fish and slightly soggy chips doused in vinegar out of white paper parcels, surrounded by seagulls with someone special sitting next to me – a perfect experience and a moment to cherish.

1   For the tartare sauce, hardboil the egg in a saucepan of simmering water for 9 minutes. Cool, then shell. Place the mayonnaise, gherkin, capers, parsley and dill in a bowl, then coarsely grate in the egg. Mix well, then season with salt and pepper to taste; the tartare should be nice and thick. Set aside. Makes 250 ml.

2   Preheat a fan-forced oven to 120°C. For the beer batter, combine the flours, bicarbonate of soda and a pinch of salt in a bowl. Pour in 75ml of the beer and whisk gently, starting from the middle, then begin to combine, drawing in the flour from the edge of the bowl. Add another 75 ml of the beer and whisk vigorously to form a smooth batter. Add the remaining beer and whisk until the batter reaches the consistency of thick cream. Set aside.

3   For the fat chips, slice each side off the unpeeled potatoes so they are straight; you will end up with a rectangular-shaped potato. Cut in half lengthways, then cut each half into 3 fat chips and place in a large saucepan. Cover with cold water and bring to the boil over high heat. Cook for 2 minutes, then drain and pat dry with paper towel. (Remember that water and hot oil don't mix, so no putting wet chips into hot fat; it is best to keep water well away.)

4   Heat the oil in a deep heavy-based saucepan over high heat until it registers 185°C on a candy thermometer or until a cube of bread browns in 4–5 seconds. Turn the heat down to low. Working in batches, fry the chips in the hot oil for 3–4 minutes or until crisp and golden. Remove and place on paper towel to drain. Transfer to a baking tray and keep warm in the oven.

5   Coat the fish with flour, patting off the excess. Drop into the batter and coat well. Lift each piece at one end, allowing the excess batter to run off. Gently lower 1 piece of fish into the hot oil, holding one end for a few seconds until the fish floats. Let go gently and cook for 4 minutes or until the batter is crisp and a light-golden brown. Drain the fish on paper towel. Repeat with the remaining pieces. Sprinkle the fish and chips with sea salt and serve with tartare sauce and lemon wedges.

Serves 6–8

500 g white fish fillets such as flake or blue grenadier, skin removed, pin-boned and cut into 10 cm × 2 cm strips
plain flour, for dusting
sea salt flakes
lemon wedges, to serve

BEER BATTER
150 g self-raising flour
150 g cornflour
½ teaspoon bicarbonate of soda
table salt
300 ml beer

TARTARE SAUCE
1 free-range egg
200 ml Basic Mayonnaise
    (see page 181)
4 gherkins, finely chopped
3 tablespoons salted capers, rinsed, drained and finely chopped
⅓ cup flat-leaf parsley, finely chopped
⅓ cup finely chopped dill
sea salt flakes and freshly ground white pepper

FAT CHIPS
4 extra-large desiree potatoes
1.5 litres vegetable oil

Notes

- *If preferred, drizzle the par-cooked chips with 80 ml olive oil and roast at 200°C for 30 minutes or until golden, turning frequently.*

- *A candy thermometer guarantees you are using a safe deep-frying temperature. Don't overcrowd the oil as it dramatically reduces its temperature and changes the result – nothing worse than soggy fish and chips.*

Grilled Marlin with Hot Olive and Anchovy Sauce

Serves 4

150 ml extra virgin olive oil
4 anchovy fillets, chopped
3 cloves garlic, thinly sliced
150 g mixed green and black olives,
    pitted and quartered
⅓ cup flat-leaf parsley, snipped
¼ cup dill, snipped
¼ cup tarragon leaves
25 g unsalted butter
2 bunches Tuscan black cabbage
    (cavolo nero), washed, bases
    trimmed, leaves shredded
sea salt flakes and freshly ground
    white pepper
squeeze of lemon juice, plus
    lemon wedges, to serve
4 × 150 g marlin steaks

Notes

• *Black cabbage or cavolo nero is a cabbage variety with lovely dense, dark-green leaves that I describe as meaty and squeaky. Dad grew it in our garden when I was a kid and I love it. Kale or shredded silverbeet leaves are a good substitute.*

• *Pitting olives is super-easy so do it yourself if you have time. Cut the olives down both sides of the pit using a small, sharp knife, then give them a gentle squeeze. The olives will give a little, which makes it easy to pull out the stones.*

I adore meaty game fish such as marlin, tuna and swordfish. It is sweet, soft, probably the least fishy of all seafood and can be eaten rare. Marlin is a perfect choice for the barbecue, but it must be seared quickly and served medium-rare to be enjoyed at its best. It dries out quickly if overcooked and, even though it's not ridiculously expensive, it would be a shame to do this to it. Salmon and Hiramasa kingfish are super substitutes for marlin in this recipe – both are very high-quality fish and our aquaculture industry in Australia is second to none.

Don't be scared of using anchovies – they are a simple, healthy way to add saltiness to food. However, it is important to use good-quality anchovies as they are certainly not all the same. The olive sauce is typical of southern Italy and also works well with chicken or even a nice piece of steak.

1   Preheat a barbecue grill-plate or cast-iron chargrill pan on high heat.

2   Heat 130 ml of the olive oil in a small saucepan over low heat until warm. Add the anchovy and two-thirds of the garlic and cook for 2 minutes or until fragrant. Add the olives and cook for a further 2 minutes to warm through. Remove from the heat, then add the herbs. Set aside.

3   Place a non-stick frying pan over medium heat, then add the butter and allow to bubble. Add the black cabbage and the remaining garlic, then season with salt and pepper. Cook for 4 minutes, stirring regularly. Add the lemon juice and set aside.

4   Brush the marlin steaks with the remaining olive oil and season with salt and pepper. Sear the marlin on the barbecue grill-plate or chargrill pan on each side for 2–3 minutes, then remove from the heat.

5   Place a marlin steak on each of 4 plates, spoon over the olive and anchovy sauce, then serve with the black cabbage and lemon wedges to the side.

Garlicky Seafood Stew

At its simplest, this lovely Italian fish stew, known as *brodetto*, contains only one or two types of fish and no shellfish or prawns. After all it is traditionally a peasant dish and need not be extravagant. The use of fennel, Pernod and dill takes it up a notch and gives the stew a lovely aniseed flavour, which works perfectly with the pungent garlic and sweet fish. Choose meatier fish such as blue-eye trevalla, monkfish or snapper for the body of the meal, as they add flavour and depth, while smaller, more subtle fish such as garfish and red mullet add interest. While fish stock is not essential, starting with a good flavour base contributes to the end result – the better the base the better the stew. However, the smell of a bubbling pot of bones (especially fish) can be a bit off-putting for some, so substitute with a good light chicken stock if you prefer.

1 Heat 90 ml of the olive oil in a saute pan or large heavy-based saucepan over high heat. Cook the onion, fennel and garlic for 3 minutes or until translucent and tinged slightly golden. Add the saffron and paprika and cook for a further 2 minutes until fragrant, then add the tomato, thyme and bay leaves and cook, stirring, for a few minutes. Add the Pernod and potato, then pour in the stock and bring to the boil. Reduce the heat to low and simmer for 20 minutes or until the potato is tender.

2 Meanwhile, to clean the calamari, rinse and then separate the hood and tentacles. Rinse and remove the contents of the hood and rinse again. Remove the head and beak from the tentacles and rinse again. Remove and discard the quill from the hood, then thinly slice the hood. Set aside.

3 Add the thickest fish chunks (that is the blue-eye) first, followed by the thinner pieces, then 2–3 minutes later add the prawns. Cover and simmer for 5 minutes, then add the clams, mussels and calamari and cook until the shellfish open; discard any unopened mussels and clams. Add a pinch of sea salt if required and season with pepper. Throw in the dill and parsley, then add the remaining olive oil. Divide between 4 bowls and enjoy with grilled bread slathered in garlicky aïoli.

Notes

- *Buy fish from a reputable fishmonger who is busy. He'll turn his stock over regularly and will be able to get hold of almost anything you want, if you ask nicely! Look for bright eyes, red gills and firm, resilient flesh in whole fish that smells of nothing but the sea. If possible, buy whole fish as the flesh close to the bone is sweeter.*

- *Clams are full of sand – they grow in it after all! Before cooking it is important to purge them in plenty of water, changing the water several times over the course of an hour.*

Serves 4

140 ml extra virgin olive oil
1 onion, thinly sliced
½ bulb fennel, trimmed, thinly sliced
5 cloves garlic, chopped
pinch of saffron
1 tablespoon smoked paprika (see page 197)
6 tomatoes, halved, seeded, roughly chopped
2 sprigs thyme
2 fresh bay leaves
50 ml Pernod (see page 196)
6 waxy potatoes (see page 196), halved
750 ml Fish Stock or Chicken Stock (see page 183)
1 calamari
1 × 200 g blue-eye trevalla fillet, skin removed, pin-boned, cut into large chunks
200 g monkfish fillets, skin removed, pin-boned, cut into large chunks
200 g red mullet fillets, skin removed, pin-boned, cut into large chunks
4 raw prawns
16 clams, soaked in water to remove the sand, washed
12 black mussels, well washed, drained, bearded
sea salt flakes and freshly ground black pepper
2 tablespoons roughly chopped dill
⅓ cup roughly chopped flat-leaf parsley
grilled crusty or sourdough bread and Pepper Aïoli (see page 131), **to serve**

Blue-eye Trevalla with Black Mussel Soup and Basil Butter

Many years ago, George Calombaris and I worked on a promotion of Australian food and produce (and Fenix Restaurant) at the Hyatt Regency Mainz in Germany, just outside Frankfurt on the Rhine River. One of the ingredients that stood out on the trip was some tiny little mussels a little smaller than the top of my thumb, imported from France each day. I fell in love with *moules marinière* (mussels in white wine) all over again. These slightly salty, plump, meaty molluscs belong in a big bowl accompanied by good beer to wash them down. In the absence of these, the mussels I have used here are from Tasmania, where they harvest them small – delish! Starting off with lots of shallots, thyme and a good-quality white wine is the secret to cooking great mussels, then cook them quickly over high heat so their shells just pop open to seal the deal.

1   For the basil butter, blend the basil and butter with a stick blender or in a small food processor until the mixture is softened, green and smooth. Season with salt and pepper. Transfer to a sheet of plastic film, then roll into a log and twist the ends to seal. Refrigerate until needed. Leftovers will keep in the fridge for a week or so, or in the freezer for up to 3 months.

2   Heat 1 tablespoon of the olive oil in a wide-based saucepan over high heat, then add the garlic, thyme, carrot, shallot and celery and cook for 3 minutes or until tender. Add the mussels and wine to the pan and pop on the lid. When the mussels start to open, remove the pan from the heat. Remove the mussels and set aside, discarding any that haven't opened. Reserve the cooking liquid and vegetables.

3   Add the cream to the pan and bring to the boil, then add the lemon juice and simmer for 2 minutes. Set aside.

4   Heat a large heavy-based non-stick frying pan over medium heat, then add the remaining olive oil and cook the fish, skin-side down, for 3–4 minutes. When the skin is crisp, turn the fish over and cook over low heat for a further 2 minutes or until cooked through. Remove and set aside.

5   Meanwhile, remove some of the mussels from the shells, if desired. Return the mussels to the soup. Add the zucchini, then bring to the boil and add 60 g of the basil butter, shaking the pan until the butter has melted and emulsified with the soup. Spoon the mussel soup into 4 bowls and place a piece of blue-eye in each bowl, then serve.

Serves 4

50 ml olive oil
1 clove garlic, finely chopped
3 sprigs thyme
1 small carrot, washed, cut into small dice
4 shallots, cut into small dice
1 stick celery, washed, cut into small dice
1 kg black mussels, well washed, drained, bearded
100 ml dry white wine
125 ml thickened cream
squeeze of lemon juice
4 × 160 g blue-eye trevalla fillets, pin-boned, skin-on, then scored
1 small zucchini, washed, cut into small dice

BASIL BUTTER
1 bunch basil, leaves picked
120 g unsalted butter, at room temperature, chopped
table salt and freshly ground white pepper

Notes

- *When buying mussels, avoid open and gaping individuals. They should close if tapped and feel heavy in proportion to their size.*

- *To add a different dimension to the soup, remove some of the strained stock. Foam it in a blender with the 60 g basil butter, then add to the pan.*

- *This versatile basil butter is a compound butter, meaning it contains more than one component. It is excellent with grilled steak or fish. Substitute watercress for basil and add 1 teaspoon wholegrain mustard.*

Pan-fried Swordfish with Lentils and Caramelised Onion

If there was ever a bistro-style dish to include in a book of my favourite comfort food recipes then this is it. Lentils du Puy are a small green lentil from Puy in France – they are gorgeous! Although you might not immediately think that lentils go with fish, they work with meatier varieties such as tuna, kingfish, marlin, or, in this case, swordfish. Because of the dense quality and meaty nature of these fish, they should be cooked to medium-rare to preserve their flavour and texture. The sweetness of the caramelised onion works wonders with the sweet meatiness of the fish. The end result is that you just want to tear up some crusty bread and dig in.

1   For the caramelised onion, place a heavy-based saucepan over medium heat. Add the olive oil and onion and cook, stirring occasionally, for 40 minutes or until the onion is very soft, sweet and a deep-brown colour. Stir through the vinegar at the very end, then remove from the heat and set aside.

2   Meanwhile, for the braised lentils, place the olive oil in a saucepan over medium heat, then cook the carrot, shallot, celery and garlic for 3 minutes, stirring occasionally. Rinse the lentils under running water, then drain and add to the pan. Add the wine and simmer for 3 minutes or until it has reduced by half. Add the stock and water and bring to the boil, then reduce the heat to low and simmer the lentils for 45 minutes or until they are tender. Set aside.

3   Heat a large heavy-based non-stick frying pan over high heat, then season the fish with salt and pepper. Add the oil to the pan, then fry the fish for 3 minutes or until golden, without turning or moving unnecessarily. Turn over and cook for another 3 minutes, then remove from the pan.

4   To serve, spoon a mound of lentils onto each bowl or plate with a little of the pan juices, then top with a swordfish steak. Put a large spoonful of caramelised onion on top of the fish, then scatter the lentils with tomato (if using) and serve with crusty bread, if desired.

Serves 4

4 × 150 g swordfish steaks, brown sinew and fat trimmed (see Notes)
sea salt flakes and freshly ground white pepper
30 ml olive oil
finely diced tomato and crusty bread (optional), to serve

BRAISED LENTILS
1 tablespoon olive oil
1 carrot, finely chopped
2 shallots, finely chopped
1 stick celery, finely chopped
1 clove garlic, chopped
200 g Puy-style green lentils
80 ml dry white wine
600 ml Veal Stock (see page 182)
1 litre water

CARAMELISED ONION
30 ml olive oil
3 onions, sliced
30 ml sherry vinegar

Notes

- *I trim the brown fat and train of sinewy flesh from the edge of the fish, forming nice, compact, round pieces. Although this is not necessary, we also eat with our eyes, don't we!*

- *Onions contain an enormous amount of natural sugars, as do carrots. This is why we use them in the bases for stews and sauces as they add that essential element of sweetness. Cooking onions slowly brings out their natural sweetness, and then increasing the heat at the end of the cooking time adds a lovely caramelised flavour.*

Snapper with Green Peppercorn and Herb Butter

Fish cooked whole is delicious, with its crisp skin and sweet flesh next to the bone; it's a real party piece that always impresses at the dinner table. The bigger the fish, the harder it is to gauge when it is cooked through, so I find that it is a good idea to start with small fish such as baby snapper, baby barramundi or trout as they are easier to deal with at home. Score the flesh at the thickest part of the fish (just behind the head) to assist the heat to penetrate and cook the fish evenly. A compound (that is flavoured) butter such as the one here is easy to make and adds a great finishing touch.

1   For the green peppercorn and herb butter, chop the butter into small pieces or blend in a blender or food processor (this makes it easier to mix with the remaining ingredients). Crush half of the peppercorns with a mortar and pestle or finely chop with a knife to extract the flavour. Blend all the ingredients in a small blender until the butter is smooth and a nice green colour. Transfer the butter to a bowl, then cover with plastic film and set aside. (If you like, you can transfer the butter to a piece of plastic film, then roll into a log-shape, wrap tightly and refrigerate.) Leftovers will keep in the fridge for a week or so or in the freezer for up to 3 months.

2   Preheat a fan-forced oven to 185°C.

3   Make three 2.5 cm long × 1 cm deep incisions on each side of the fish at the thickest part, starting from just behind the gills. Heat the oil in an ovenproof chargrill pan or flameproof heavy-based non-stick roasting pan over high heat. Gently place the fish in the pan, then transfer to the oven to bake for 4 minutes. (It is not essential, but I like to turn the fish at this stage. However, if you are not comfortable doing this or are concerned the fish may break, brush the tops with a little of the oil in the base of the pan.) Return to the oven to cook for another 4–5 minutes or until the fish are cooked through. To test, when you press your finger onto the thickest part of a fish it should give slightly. Otherwise, insert the tip of a knife and have a look; the flesh should be opaque.

4   Season the snapper with salt and pepper, then place one on each of 4 plates and top with a slice or spoonful of the green peppercorn and herb butter. Serve with lemon wedges and rocket to the side.

Serves 4

4 × 300 g baby snapper, cleaned and scaled with fins removed
60 ml olive oil
sea salt flakes and freshly ground black pepper
lemon wedges and rocket, to serve

GREEN PEPPERCORN AND HERB BUTTER
250 g unsalted butter, softened
⅓ cup soft green peppercorns, rinsed
¼ cup finely chopped chervil
¼ cup finely chopped dill
¼ cup chopped flat-leaf parsley

Notes

- *When you scale a fish feel free to wash it to remove all those loose scales, then pat it dry with paper towel. If filleting it, wipe your chopping board and knife, then start to fillet it away from the sink. I was once told that you wouldn't think of washing a nice steak under the tap, so don't wash fish fillets – I see it often and it drives me crazy!*

- *All butters are not equal – cheap butter is most often bulk-imported and frozen at some stage, so beware. Try different brands and choose unsalted butter over salted; it should be creamy but clean and milky in taste. Butter goes rancid fairly quickly if left out of the fridge and, more importantly, when exposed to air.*

Grilled Prawns with Chilli and Fennel and Pepper Aïoli

Serves 4

16 raw prawns
1 teaspoon fennel seeds
30 ml olive oil, plus extra
    for drizzling
2 fresh long thin red chillies,
    thinly sliced
2 cloves garlic, thinly sliced
table salt and freshly ground
    white pepper
¼ cup coriander, thinly sliced
lime wedges, to serve

PEPPER AÏOLI
1 small potato, washed
½ cup rock salt
1 head garlic
125 ml Basic Mayonnaise (see page 181)
table salt and 1 teaspoon freshly
    ground black pepper
finely grated zest and juice of 1 lime

Notes

• *Baking the potato on rock salt helps to transfer the heat evenly through the potato while drawing moisture away from the point of contact with the pan. It also gives you a dry, fluffy-textured potato — the perfect starting point for mash, gnocchi and, in this case, aïoli.*

• *Roasting the garlic before adding it to the aïoli brings out its natural sweetness, softening the pungent bite for which garlic is renowned.*

When it comes to food, there is nothing more quintessentially Australian than prawns on the barbie. I am old enough to remember Paul Hogan's adverts of sunny Oz when I still lived in England — a prawn as big as the one in that ad is unheard of to the Brits. What we have here is very special, so buy the best, freshest (that is sulphur-free) Australian prawns that you can find. Prawns should smell beautiful, like the sea — any hint of ammonia is associated with old seafood so if in doubt, steer clear. Also avoid prawns with any sign of black in the heads as this is a sure sign that they are well past their best. Find a fishmonger you trust and one that is always super-busy!

I like to butterfly prawns then cook them this way as it allows you to add flavourings such as spices while keeping them sweet and moist by retaining the shell. And yes, I do eat the shell (not all, but most of it) but it's up to you! An old Japanese tepanyaki trick is to pop the heads back on the grill-plate and toast them until crisp, then eat them.

1   Preheat a fan-forced oven to 180°C.

2   For the aïoli, bake the potato on a bed of rock salt in a small roasting pan for 30 minutes. Place the garlic next to the potato and bake for 30 minutes. While the garlic and potato are still hot, remove the flesh from the potato and squeeze the soft garlic from the skin. Immediately press the potato and garlic through a sieve into a bowl or mash them together. While still warm, add the mayonnaise and whisk until combined. Season with salt to taste and the pepper. Add the lime zest and juice. Set aside. Makes about 250 ml.

3   Split the prawns from the under-side with a sharp knife or kitchen scissors (often it's easier to use kitchen scissors to split the heads), then cut carefully along the belly with the tip of a knife. If you prefer, remove the heads and split the tails only. Remove the digestive tract, then gently press the prawns flat to expose the flesh. Sprinkle the flesh-side of each prawn with the fennel seeds, olive oil, chilli and garlic, then season with salt and pepper.

4   Heat a chargrill pan or barbecue grill-plate over high heat until hot. Place the prawns flesh-side down onto the pan or grill-plate, then lightly press to ensure contact with the pan. Grill the prawns for 3 minutes or until lightly golden, then turn and cook for a further 2 minutes until cooked through.

5   Drizzle the prawns with olive oil, sprinkle with coriander and serve with the aïoli and lime wedges to the side.

Chilli Crab

Take a trip to Singapore or Malaysia and eat chilli crab – forget the shopping and become a food tourist. There is nothing like sitting in thirty degrees Celsius heat with ninety per cent humidity over a bowl of steaming hot (and chilli hot) crab and working your way through the claws, legs and shells with a bib tucked high around your neck. With the sweat beading on your forehead, it's hard work, but it's a great food experience, accompanied by the cathedral-like silence that a brilliant dish inspires. I have tried many crab recipes with all sorts of sauces, but give me a bib, finger bowl, beer and crab cooked this way and I am a happy man. This recipe for chilli crab is my favourite so I encourage you to give it a go.

1   Place the crabs in the freezer to slow their metabolism for 1 hour. Place them top-side down on a chopping board, then quickly cut in half lengthways with a cleaver or large heavy knife. Cut into quarters, then crack the claws with the back of a large knife. Remove the top shell from the body and discard the 'dead man's fingers' (feathery gills that run along either side of the crab's body – you will see them when the top shell is removed).

2   Puree 7 of the chillies, the onion, ginger and garlic in a blender or food processor.

3   Heat a wok over medium heat, then pour in the oil. Stir in the onion puree and belachan and cook, stirring, for 3–4 minutes or until fragrant and soft. Stir in the coconut vinegar, tomato, tomato paste and sugar. Simmer for 2 minutes, then add the tomato sauce, soy sauce and lemongrass. Add the crab and bring to a gentle simmer, then cook for 10 minutes or until it is cooked through. Add the water if required to keep the mixture loose and bubbling, stirring occasionally.

4   Meanwhile, chop the remaining chilli. Stir in the egg at the last minute until just cooked, add the chopped chilli, spring onion and coriander. Serve with bibs and enjoy!

Serves 4

2 mud crabs
8 fresh long thin red chillies
1 onion, roughly chopped
1 knob young ginger
4 cloves garlic, thinly sliced
90 ml olive oil
1 teaspoon belachan (see page 194)
1 tablespoon coconut vinegar
  (see page 195)
1 × 400 g tin chopped tomato
2 tablespoons tomato paste
75 g grated palm sugar
200 ml tomato sauce
100 ml soy sauce
1 stick lemongrass, white part
  only, finely chopped
350 ml water (optional, as needed)
1 free-range egg, lightly beaten
6 spring onions, thinly sliced
  on the diagonal
⅓ cup coriander leaves

Notes

· *If you can't get hold of mud crabs, then use blue swimmer crabs instead – they are not as meaty but have a beautiful, soft, sweet flesh.*

· *To differentiate between male and female mud crabs, the females have a much broader, rounder abdominal flap. The males have larger claws, which make them good eating. Only male crabs can be harvested by fishermen and they have to meet a minimum size standard to secure their future on the table.*

· *Grating or finely chopping palm sugar helps it to dissolve more easily – there is nothing worse than big lumps of sugar in your chilli crab!*

Warm Breton Cake with Poached Mandarins

There are a number of recipes out there for butter cakes and Breton cakes – and this one may be a combination of the two. I've been cooking this version for years and it's great either made in a large tin as I've done here (see opposite) or pressed into the holes of a muffin tray or small stainless-steel rings that help the batter hold its shape in the oven. Because this is such a short (that is, buttery) mixture, the cake tends to sink a little in the centre after you remove it from the oven. Don't worry, this is because it is so rich and soft – so relax and prepare to enjoy! Let's be frank – this is not a slimming recipe and it contains more butter than most of us would likely eat in a month – but my goodness does it taste good. Served with poached mandarins or eaten warm on its own with a nice pot of tea it takes me to another place – one where butter is king!

1. For the poached mandarins, rub the sugar cubes over 4 of the mandarins and set aside. Juice 6 of the mandarins. Bring the mandarin juice, sugar cubes, sugar, star anise, cinnamon, cloves and liqueur to the boil in a saucepan over high heat, then reduce the heat to low and simmer, stirring, for 3–4 minutes or until the sugar has dissolved. Meanwhile, peel the remaining 6 mandarins, removing as much of the pith as possible with your fingers. Immerse the mandarins in the simmering syrup, then simmer for 10 minutes over low heat. Remove the pan from the heat and leave the mandarins to cool in the syrup.

2. Beat the yolks and the sugar in a bowl with hand-held electric beaters until pale and fluffy. Add the softened butter and continue to beat until fully incorporated. Sift the flour and baking powder into a bowl, then add it to the butter mixture and combine into a soft, cohesive dough with a wooden spoon. Transfer the dough to a lightly floured surface and roll into a thick 5 cm-thick log. Wrap tightly in plastic film and chill in the fridge for 30 minutes.

3. Preheat a fan-forced oven to 165°C. Lightly grease a 24 cm springform cake tin.

4. Press the dough into the prepared tin, using your fingers to form an even layer. Run the tines of a fork across the surface of the dough to create shallow ridges. Brush with the beaten egg. Bake for 35 minutes or until golden. Cool a little before serving.

5. Serve slices of the warm Breton cake with poached mandarins, a drizzle of syrup and a dollop of double cream.

Serves 6

3 free-range egg yolks
160 g caster sugar
160 g unsalted butter, softened
225 g plain flour, plus extra for dusting
1 tablespoon baking powder
1 free-range egg, lightly beaten
double cream, to serve

POACHED MANDARINS
100 g sugar cubes
12 mandarins, washed and dried
300 g caster sugar
4 star anise
1 cinnamon stick, halved lengthways
4 cloves
20 ml mandarin Napoleon
    liqueur or brandy

Notes

- Because the butter is such an integral part of this cake, buy a good-quality, fresh, unsalted butter – it will make all the difference to the final result.

- You can make the dough, roll it into a log, then wrap it in plastic wrap and store it in the fridge for up to 7 days or freezer for up to 3 months.

- To make small cakes, divide the dough between smaller moulds such as the holes of a muffin tray or cupcake tin, then reduce the cooking time accordingly – check after 8 minutes.

Good Old English Doughnuts with Raspberry Jam and Lavender Sugar

When I was about seven or eight years old we used to have a 'bread man' who would turn up on our street with a van full of freshly baked breads, buns and tarts as well as sugary doughnuts full of jam. He had a white coat, kept his money in an old leather satchel and wore a big smile. If we were lucky (and we begged Mum enough), two of the best doughnuts in the world were bestowed upon my sister and me. Sadly the bread man and milkman have gone the way of the dodo, but the memory of the smell of that gorgeous bread and the taste of those fresh doughnuts have not!

1 Heat the butter and milk in a saucepan over low heat until it reaches blood temperature (just warm). Pour into a bowl, then add the sugar and yeast and stir until dissolved. Whisk the eggs into the milk mixture.

2 Put the flour and salt into a large bowl. Create a well in the centre, then tip the egg mixture into the well. Whisk the flour and egg mixture together, starting from the centre and drawing in the flour until a smooth, thick batter forms. Cover the bowl with a tea towel or plastic film and put in a warm spot to rise for 1 hour or until half the volume again.

3 Transfer the dough to a piping bag fitted with a large nozzle. Tie the end of the bag, allowing enough room at the end for the dough to double in volume, then leave for 45 minutes or until the bag is firm and taut.

4 For the lavender sugar, rub the lavender flowers with the sugar until the leaves have broken up and the sugar is fragrant; discard the stalks. Set aside.

5 Heat the vegetable oil in a large heavy-based saucepan or domestic deep-fryer to 185°C or until a cube of bread browns in 4–5 seconds. Working in batches so as not to crowd the pan, pipe out small balls (about 1 tablespoon) of the dough directly into the hot oil and cook for 4 minutes or until golden, turning once or twice during cooking. Lift the doughnuts out with a slotted spoon and drain on paper towel.

6 Prick a hole in each doughnut with the tip of a small sharp knife, then pipe a little raspberry jam into each one. Roll each doughnut in the lavender sugar. Serve immediately with clotted or double cream.

Serves 4

50 g unsalted butter, chopped
220 ml milk
30 g caster sugar
1 × 7 g sachet dried yeast
2 free-range eggs
300 g plain flour
pinch of table salt
1 litre vegetable oil
100 g raspberry jam
clotted or double cream, to serve

LAVENDER SUGAR
10 unsprayed lavender flowers
150 g caster sugar

Notes

- *If you don't have a piping bag, gently push tablespoonfuls of the dough into the hot oil with your index finger.*

- *A candy thermometer is a cheap investment in safety when deep-frying. It gives you confidence that the oil temperature is spot-on and allows you to adjust it to achieve the best results.*

- *Yeast helps dough rise best in a warm, moist environment. In winter, use a microwave oven or turned off regular oven with a pan of steaming hot water placed inside, then put the dough inside and shut the door. This creates the perfect conditions for yeast to work.*

Bakewell Tart

When I was growing up in England, the Mr Kipling brand of Bakewell tarts used to advertise on telly and their catchphrase was, 'Exceedingly good cakes'. In a house with few sweet things, they always looked amazing. I was guilty of stopping at a little corner shop to buy a packet of these tarts on my way home from school, then scoffing the lot during the final leg of my walk home (I am sure this is where my inability to resist food started!). When I began working in London I moved in with my aunty. I remember that she made Bakewell tarts twice a week – I am sure she was worried about all those hours I worked and feared that I may fade away under her guardianship. I lived with her for just three months, but it was long enough to realise that there was more to Bakewell tarts than the packaged ones in that little corner shop. Thanks Aunty Irene!

1   Grease a 28 cm tart tin with a removable base. To line the tin with the dough, peel off one sheet of baking paper and then turn it, dough-side down, over the tart tin. Gently ease the dough into the tin. Remove and reserve the remaining paper, then mould the pastry up the sides of the tin with your fingertips. Remove any excess pastry with your thumbs by pressing down along the edge of tin, crimping the pastry as you go, if desired. Chill in the fridge for 30 minutes.

2   Preheat a fan-forced oven to 160°C.

3   Press the sheet of reserved baking paper onto the pastry, then fill with rice or baking beans and blind bake for 15 minutes or until golden. Remove from the oven, then remove the rice or baking beans and baking paper and leave to cool. Spread the cooled pastry base with a 5 mm-thick layer of strawberry jam.

4   Cream the butter and sugar in a large bowl with hand-held electric beaters until pale and fluffy, then add the eggs and egg yolk one at a time while continuing to mix. Add the almond essence, lemon zest, ground almonds and flour and mix to combine. Spoon the almond mixture into the pastry case to fill to the top, then level the surface with the back of a spoon. Bake for 15 minutes. Remove from the oven and sprinkle with the flaked almonds. Return to the oven and cook for a further 25 minutes or until golden.

5   Dust the tart with icing sugar and serve warm or at room temperature.

Serves 8–10

1 quantity Basic Sweet Pastry
   (see page 185)
good-quality strawberry jam,
   for spreading
180 g unsalted butter, chopped
180 g caster sugar
3 free-range eggs, plus 1 yolk
few drops of almond essence
finely grated zest of 1 lemon
180 g ground almonds
60 g plain flour
flaked almonds and icing sugar,
   to serve

Notes

- *For an alternative frangipane (almond mixture), mix 100 g ground almonds, 30 g plain flour and 100 g caster sugar. Add 3 egg whites and mix until smooth. Heat 30 g unsalted butter in a saucepan over medium heat until melted and nut-brown in colour, then pour into the flour mixture and add 50 ml Amaretto. Mix together and proceed with the recipe.*

Rich Chocolate
and Nut Brownies

I originally tested a chocolate tart recipe to include in this book when I came across this brownie in an old recipe book of mine. Sure I've embellished it with a little extra chocolate and nuts and maybe even a tad too much sugar – but wait until you try it. These brownies are soft, gooey and everything ridiculously chocolate-y that a brownie should be – no need to explain further why they replaced the tart!

Bake half a quantity of the batter if you feel you lack self-control because you're going to need it. If by chance there are some leftover, pop them into an airtight container for later; just blast them in the microwave for fifteen seconds before eating. I also find that a generous dollop of ice cream seems to improve things no end – a brownie, my mood and life in general!

1 Preheat a fan-forced oven to 160°C.

2 Grease and line a 24 cm × 21 cm lamington tin with baking paper.

3 Melt the butter in a small saucepan over medium heat. Place the sugar, cocoa powder and melted butter in a mixing bowl and beat with hand-held electric beaters. Whisk in the eggs one at a time. In a separate bowl, sift the flour and baking powder together, then fold through the cocoa mixture. Mix the chocolate and peanuts in another bowl and then fold them through the batter.

4 Pour the batter into the prepared tin and bake for 20–25 minutes or until cooked through; the brownie should be soft and gooey in the centre. Leave to cool in the tin a little to firm before slicing. Dust with extra cocoa powder and serve warm or at room temperature with a nice big dob of ice cream or cream.

Makes 12

250 g unsalted butter, chopped
515 g caster sugar
90 g dutch-process cocoa powder (see page 195), **plus extra for dusting**
5 free-range eggs
150 g plain flour
½ teaspoon baking powder
175 g dark couverture chocolate (see page 194), **chopped**
75 g unsalted roasted peanuts, chopped
ice cream or whipped cream, to serve

Notes

- *The simplest way to melt chocolate is over a pan of boiling water. Break the chocolate into small pieces, then place in a clean, dry, heatproof bowl. Bring the water to the boil, turn off the heat, then place the bowl over the pan. It is not necessary to keep the water boiling, and there is a risk that the increased steam will fall into the chocolate and spoil it. The residual heat will melt the chocolate gently, so just stir occasionally.*

- *Make sure the oven is preheated to the specified temperature before baking the brownie. Depending on your oven it may take up to 40 minutes or so to cook.*

- *Although it is hard to resist, a good cake is not at its best until it has cooled. Leave it in the tin or mould until it is easy to handle, then turn it out onto a wire rack to cool further.*

Jam Roly-Poly with Custard

Jam roly-poly reminds me of my childhood – I can't resist it. Mum used to make a great jam roly-poly with loads of her own strawberry jam and thick custard. I hope I have done her proud.

1   Mix the self-raising flour, sugar and suet mix in a large bowl with your hands. Make a well in the centre and pour in the water, then gently draw the flour into the centre with your fingers. It may need a little extra water, so judge this yourself – you are looking for a soft-textured dough. The secret is not to overwork the dough. Turn the dough onto a lightly floured surface and gently shape it into a ball. Press the dough down with your fingers to create a rectangular shape, then transfer it to a 60 cm × 60 cm sheet of baking paper. Dust with a little flour and roll out until 1 cm-thick, leaving a 6 cm border of paper.

2   Use a spatula to spread the dough liberally with jam, leaving the top 3–4 cm jam-free. Wet this top edge with a little water. Starting at the bottom edge, start to roll the pastry away from you all the way to the top. Slide the jam roly-poly back towards you until it reaches the bottom edge of the baking paper. At this point, slide the baking paper and jam roly-poly onto a clean tea towel. Roll it all up loosely; this allows the pastry to expand during cooking. Tie the ends of the tea towel together with kitchen twine to seal.

3   Place the jam roly-poly in a saucepan steamer insert. Fill the saucepan with 4 cm water, then bring to the boil over high heat. Place the steamer insert on top of the pan, then cover with the lid and steam for 45 minutes.

4   For the custard, bring the milk and vanilla pod to the boil in a saucepan. Meanwhile, whisk the egg yolks and sugar until pale and fluffy, then whisk in the cornflour. Pour the hot milk into the egg mixture, then pour the lot back into the saucepan and whisk continuously over high heat until it thickens.

5   To check if the roly-poly is ready, insert a skewer into the centre of the roll – it should come out clean and feel hot. Remove the roly-poly from the steamer, then unwrap it and cut it into slices. Serve slices of the roly-poly with lashings of custard.

Serves 4–6

200 g self-raising flour
30 g caster sugar
200 g suet mix (see page 197)
200 ml water, approximately
plain flour, for dusting
60 g good-quality strawberry jam
kitchen twine

CUSTARD
500 ml milk
½ vanilla pod, split
5 free-range egg yolks
90 g caster sugar
50 g cornflour

Notes

- *You will need a steamer insert that fits snugly over a saucepan for cooking roly-poly. If you don't have one a bamboo steamer is the perfect substitute – they are cheap and easy to use.*

- *If your steamer is not big enough, you can make two small roly-polys instead; just be sure to reduce the cooking time accordingly, checking them after 25 minutes.*

- *Making your first real custard is a bit of a thrill because it is so easy and tastes brilliant in comparison to the packaged stuff (and everyone will think you are pretty clever!).*

Lemon Verbena Custard Tart

Serves 8

1 quantity Basic Sweet Pastry
(see page 185)
6 lemon verbena leaves
80 ml milk
200 ml pouring cream
2 free-range eggs
1 free-range egg yolk
50 g caster sugar
1 teaspoon cornflour
freshly grated nutmeg, to serve

Note

- *For a lavender-scented custard filling, use fresh unsprayed lavender flowers instead of lemon verbena. Pick the tips of the lavender and rub them into the sugar with your fingertips, then put them into a small saucepan with the milk and heat over low heat, stirring, until the sugar has dissolved. Leave to cool for about 30 minutes. Strain the milk, discarding the flowers, and proceed with making the custard as described opposite.*

- *If preferred, you can replace the lemon verbena leaves with grated orange or lemon zest.*

A nice custard tart is hard to beat and I am a big fan. Its success is based on a thin, crumbly, slightly sweet pastry, but it's also important to have a soft custard filling with a hint of nutmeg or lemon. Lemon verbena has a beautiful flavour that reminds me of the lemon-flavoured boiled sweets I had as a kid. Although this recipe may be a little English, my love of custard tarts is international. During a trip to Lisbon a few years ago, a visit to Café Pasteis de Belem saw me wolf down more than a few Portuguese custard tarts – heaven! A trip to Hong Kong revealed bright-yellow, ever-so-slightly wobbly custard tarts encased in a soft pastry at Tai Cheong Bakery on Lyndhurst Terrace, Central – as much as I love them I'm lucky they are not local or I'd be the size of a house!

1   Grease a 28 cm square or round tart tin with a removable base. To line the tin with the dough, peel off one sheet of the paper and then turn it, dough-side down, over the tart tin. Gently ease the dough into the tin. Remove and reserve the remaining paper, then mould the pastry up the sides of the tin with your fingertips, reserving the baking paper. Remove any excess pastry with your thumbs by pressing down along the edge of tin. Chill in the fridge for 30 minutes.

2   Preheat a fan-forced oven to 160°C.

3   Press the sheet of baking paper onto the pastry, then fill with rice or baking beans and blind bake for 15 minutes or until golden. Remove from the oven, then remove the rice or the baking beans and baking paper and leave the pastry case to cool. Reduce the oven temperature to 130°C.

4   Gently bring the lemon verbena, milk and cream to the boil in a small saucepan over medium heat. Remove from the heat, then leave to cool for 5 minutes, whisking once or twice to help it cool slightly. Whisk the eggs, egg yolk, sugar and cornflour in a bowl until creamy. Strain the milk mixture, discarding the lemon verbena, then pour it into the egg mixture and whisk together; do not over-whisk to avoid creating air bubbles. Pour the custard into the cooled tart base and bake for 30 minutes.

5   To test if the custard is cooked, tap the side of the tin – the custard should wobble only once. Leave the tart to cool in the tin before removing. Grate a little nutmeg over the tart, then serve.

Lemon Curd Mousse with Gingernut Crumble

I have never been a big fan of cheesecake, especially the baked variety – I find them too heavy and claggy. On the other hand, this recipe is a beauty, turning the traditional idea of cheesecake on its head, with a fluffy, light and citrus-y cream cheese filling on the bottom, topped with a crisp crumble 'base'.

1 Preheat a fan-forced oven to 180°C.

2 For the crumble, beat the butter, sugar, treacle and egg yolk in a bowl until combined. Add the flour, bicarbonate of soda, ginger, star anise and cinnamon. Using your hands, combine the ingredients to form a firm dough. Turn the dough onto a lightly floured surface, then rub through with your fingertips to make large 'crumbs' and spread onto a baking tray lined with baking paper. Bake for 8 minutes or until golden. Remove from the oven and set aside to cool.

3 For the lemon curd, place the lemon juice, zest, eggs, sugar and butter in a microwave-proof bowl and microwave on medium for 6–8 minutes, stopping to stir regularly until the mixture is thick. Transfer to a clean airtight container and seal. Lemon curd will keep in the fridge for up to 2 weeks. Makes 250 ml.

4 Whisk the cream cheese in a large bowl until soft and smooth, then add the cream and condensed milk and whisk until thick and creamy; the longer you whisk, the lighter and creamier it will be. Add the citrus zest, juice and 150 ml of the lemon curd and whisk for a few seconds only.

5 Spoon the mousse into 6 glasses, sprinkle with the gingernut crumble, top with a few chopped pistachios and serve.

Notes

· *My Mum has made lemon curd for as long as I can remember and, for nearly as long, she has used the microwave. As a young chef I thought this a little too domestic – little did I know how easy it was! As long as you stir the lemon curd often there's little that can go wrong, providing you use fresh lemon juice and super-fresh eggs. Mum often uses it to whip up a nice lemon meringue pie that, between me and Dad, doesn't last long.*

· *Leftover gingernut crumble can be kept in an airtight container for up to 1 week or frozen for up to 3 months and warmed in the oven before serving.*

Serves 6

150 g cream cheese,
    at room temperature
250 ml double cream
200 g condensed milk
finely grated zest and
    juice of 1 lemon
finely grated zest and
    juice of 1 lime
chopped pistachios, to serve

LEMON CURD
180 ml lemon juice
finely grated zest of 1 lemon
5 free-range eggs
165 g caster sugar
125 g unsalted butter, chopped

GINGERNUT CRUMBLE
65 g unsalted butter, chopped
    and softened
50 g soft brown sugar
1 tablespoon treacle
1 free-range egg yolk
185 g self-raising flour,
    plus extra for dusting
½ teaspoon bicarbonate of soda
1 tablespoon ground ginger
1 teaspoon ground star anise
1 teaspoon ground cinnamon

Eton Mess with Poached Rhubarb

Eton mess is a lovely, classic, summer English dessert using cream, meringues and, traditionally, fresh berries. It is always a winner. The various components can be popped in layers into individual glasses like mini trifles or served in a big bowl at the centre of the table. The secret is to make sure all the components taste fantastic individually before mixing them together.

1   Preheat a fan-forced oven to 60°C. Line a baking tray with baking paper.

2   Place the egg whites and 50 g of the sugar in a large stainless-steel bowl and whisk with hand-held electric beaters on high until soft peaks form. Turn the beaters to low, then sprinkle in another 150 g of the sugar. Turn the beaters back to high and mix for a further 3–4 minutes until the mixture is smooth and glossy. Spoon large dollops of meringue onto the baking paper-lined tray. Bake for a minimum of 4 hours or until the surface is crisp and dry to the touch. Turn the oven off, leaving the door slightly ajar, then leave for another 4 hours or overnight.

3   Spread the rhubarb evenly in one layer over the base of a wide-based saucepan, then sprinkle with the remaining sugar. Leave to macerate for 15 minutes to draw the juices out; the rhubarb should now be sitting in a little of its own juice. Gently cook over low heat for 10 minutes or until tender; avoid stirring the rhubarb to prevent it from breaking up.

4   Whisk the cream, mascarpone and vanilla seeds in a bowl to form soft peaks. Place spoonfuls of the cream mixture into a large bowl, then break the meringues into large chunks and place on top. Spoon the rhubarb and a little of its juice onto the meringue. Stir gently with a large metal spoon 2–3 times only to swirl the components together, then serve in a clean bowl or individual glasses.

Serves 4

4 free-range egg whites,
    at room temperature
260 g caster sugar
3 large sticks rhubarb, washed,
    trimmed and cut into
    2.5 cm lengths
200 ml thickened cream
200 g mascarpone
1 vanilla pod, scraped seeds only

Notes

- *To keep meringues lovely and white they need to dry rather than bake, so the lower the oven temperature the better. However, I am not a fan of super-dry, crumbly meringues. I prefer a soft, chewy centre, so, if in doubt, break one open to check – it's a nice sweet snack if nothing else!*

- *Although meringues freeze well they do become chewy, which you either like or don't, it's up to you. Just keep the kids out of the freezer once they find them in there!*

- *Macerating the rhubarb draws out its natural juice. No need, then, to add water to the pan, which means a better (more concentrated) flavour and the rhubarb holds its shape.*

- *Depending on the season, fresh blackcurrants, raspberries, strawberries, peaches and nectarines are all perfect fruits to use instead of rhubarb.*

Hazelnut Pots with Autumn Leaves

Serves 4

400 ml pouring cream
100 ml milk
50 g caster sugar
50 g hazelnut praline paste or
    pistachio paste (see page 196)
1 free-range egg
4 free-range egg yolks

AUTUMN LEAVES
1 sheet prepared butter puff pastry
    (20 cm × 20 cm), thawed, cut in
    half lengthways
1 egg white, lightly beaten
100 g icing sugar
1 teaspoon plain flour, for dusting

Notes

• Look for a good-quality prepared butter-puff pastry, which generally comes in a single sheet (try Carême brand). This makes all the difference because cheap puff pastry is not made with butter, and is tougher, thinner and tastes inferior.

• For orange-flavoured autumn leaves, sprinkle a little finely grated orange zest on the pastry before you roll and bake it.

• Leftover almond leaves will keep in an airtight container for up to 3 days. The raw autumn leaves can be placed between 2 sheets of baking paper and frozen for up to 3 months, then thawed and baked following the instructions opposite. They can also be used to accompany poached fruit or, with a little creativity, can be the centrepiece to a special dessert in their own right.

I used to make these sugar biscuits, known as autumn leaves, years ago at The Connaught Hotel London. They are so thin and crisp that once you start eating them, you can't stop. Much like what the French refer to as a palmier, they need a little practice to perfect but are worth the effort.

1   Preheat a fan-forced oven to 120°C.

2   Bring the cream, milk, sugar and nut paste to the boil in a heavy-based saucepan over high heat, then reduce the heat to low, stirring to break up the nut paste as it dissolves. Stir the egg and yolks together in a bowl, then slowly whisk in the hot nut-paste mixture. Strain the mixture into a jug and then divide it between four 150 ml-capacity ramekins and place them in a deep roasting pan.

3   Put the pan on an oven shelf, then add enough boiling water to reach one-quarter of the way up the sides of the dishes. Cover the pan tightly with foil and bake for 30–40 minutes or until the mixture just sets; they are ready when it wobbles slightly when you shake the dish. Remove the pots from the water bath and leave to cool at room temperature, then refrigerate.

4   For the autumn leaves, place the pastry halves on a lightly floured bench with their short edge closest to you. Brush with egg white, then sprinkle 30 g of the sugar evenly across both pieces. Tightly roll each piece from the bottom edge up to the top to form a roll, then wrap each roll firmly in plastic film. Place them on a baking tray lined with baking paper in the fridge for 1 hour.

5   Preheat the oven to 180°C.

6   Remove the pastry rolls from the fridge, unwrap and cut each roll into eight 1 cm-thick rounds. Sprinkle 1 tablespoon of the icing sugar on the bench. Place a round of pastry, cut-side down, onto the sugar, then sprinkle with a further 1 tablespoon sugar. Roll a rolling pin over each pastry round to create an elongated 1 mm-thick shape. Transfer to the baking tray lined with baking paper. Repeat with the remaining pastry and icing sugar. Leave to rest in the fridge for 10 minutes. Bake for 4 minutes or until golden. Turn the leaves over. Return to the oven and bake for a further 3 minutes. Leave to cool on the tray. Makes 16.

7   Serve the hazelnut pots with autumn leaves to the side.

Raspberry Sorbet

I have included recipes for my three favourite flavours of ices in this book: caramel ice cream (see page 191); lemon mascarpone ice cream (see page 190) and raspberry sorbet. If there were to be a fourth and a fifth added they would have to be creamy rice ice cream and pistachio ice cream – the next book for those I think. Ices are always a winner for dessert. Restaurateurs also love them as they form such an integral part of more complicated desserts on their menus – I couldn't live without them.

1   Bring the water and sugar to the boil in a small saucepan over high heat. Remove from the heat and set aside to cool.

2   Blend the lemon zest, juice and raspberries in a blender or food processor until smooth, then add the sugar syrup and blend for another 30 seconds to incorporate. Push the puree through a fine mesh strainer or sieve over a bowl to remove the seeds.

3   Pour the mixture into an ice cream machine and churn until thick and smooth, following the manufacturer's instructions. If you don't have an ice cream machine, place the sieved raspberry mixture in a bowl in the freezer for a couple of hours, whisking every 45 minutes or so until frozen.

4   Blend in a food processor quickly to break up the icy lumps and return to the freezer for several hours to freeze into a sorbet. Serve scoops of sorbet in bowls or glasses.

Makes 500 ml

150 ml water
150 g caster sugar
finely grated zest and juice
**   of 1 lemon**
400 g frozen or fresh raspberries

Notes

- *Sorbets can become icy and hard if left in the freezer for a long time (that is, several days or weeks). It is best to transfer it from the freezer to the fridge to soften for 30 minutes before serving. Alternatively, you can mash or scrape the sorbet with a fork and serve it as a granita, which has a coarser, icier texture.*

- *Frozen raspberries are one of the best frozen fruits around and, when blended for sorbet or other puree-based desserts, are almost impossible to distinguish from all but the softest, sweetest, seasonal fresh raspberries.*

- *A nice tip for making raspberry puree is to first place the frozen raspberries in a dish or tray and sprinkle them with icing sugar. Leave them to thaw and let the icing sugar leach some of the delicious juice from the fruit, then blend the lot and serve.*

Friar's Omelette

I first cooked this dessert when I worked as a commis chef in the pastry section of The Connaught Hotel at the age of eighteen – I thought it was great then and I still do. As with most old-school English desserts, this one is simple and unfussy. Be generous with the breadcrumbs and buy good-quality apples – that means ones that are tasty! When I was growing up my Grandad had a big apple tree full of these ugly-looking apples that were so tart they were impossible to eat raw, but when cooked in apple pies, puddings or a friar's omelette, they were heaven. Sadly, I haven't seen such apples for more than twenty years now.

1   Bring the apple, lemon zest, juice and water to the boil in a saucepan over high heat. Reduce the heat to low and simmer, covered, for 8 minutes or until soft. Remove from the heat, then add the butter and 50 g of the sugar. Mash or puree the apple mixture in a food processor. Leave to cool. When cold, stir in the eggs.

2   Preheat a fan-forced oven to 180°C.

3   Grease a deep 1 litre-capacity baking dish with the extra butter and spread two-thirds of the breadcrumbs generously around so that they stick to the base and sides. Spoon in the apple and egg mixture and cover with the remaining breadcrumbs.

4   Bake for 30 minutes or until golden. Sprinkle with the remaining sugar, then serve with whipped cream.

Serves 4

6 golden delicious apples, peeled, cored, sliced
finely grated zest and juice of 1 lemon
150 ml water
100 g unsalted butter, chopped, plus extra for greasing
80 g white sugar
2 × 55 g free-range eggs, well beaten
70 g fresh coarse breadcrumbs
whipped cream, to serve

Notes

- *This dessert is incredibly easy to make and, depending on the season, the addition of plums, rhubarb or berries offers a pleasant change.*

- *Fresh breadcrumbs (not too fine) and a good-quality butter make for a lovely sweet and crisp crust.*

- *To make individual serves, use four 150 ml-capacity ramekins instead of a large baking dish, then reduce the cooking time accordingly – check after 10–15 minutes.*

Rich Creamy Rice Pudding with Strawberry Jam

Serves 4

200 g short-grain rice
850 ml milk, plus 150 ml extra
    if needed
½ vanilla pod, split
3 free-range egg yolks
100 g caster sugar
⅓ cup good-quality strawberry jam

I love a bowl of creamy rice pudding. This version is from my days at The Connaught Hotel kitchens in London. It is extra-rich, super-smooth and almost impossible not to go back for seconds. Make sure you top each serve with a dollop of homemade jam – it really makes all the difference to this comforting dessert.

1   Place the rice, milk and vanilla pod in a large heavy-based saucepan. Bring to the boil, then simmer over low heat for 45 minutes or until the rice is tender. Stir regularly otherwise the milk and rice will stick to the base of the pan and may burn; add a little more milk if required to keep the mixture soft and creamy. As the rice becomes soft towards the end of cooking (after about 40 minutes), whisk the egg yolks and sugar in a bowl until pale and creamy. Remove the rice from the heat and pour it into the bowl of egg mixture, then combine, stirring quickly with a flexible spatula.

2   Serve the hot rice pudding in bowls, topped with a dollop of homemade strawberry jam.

Notes

- When I revisit this recipe it always surprises me how much milk the rice absorbs, so remember to stir it regularly over the lowest possible heat and avoid adding the sugar until the end as it inhibits the cooking process and may make the rice burn more easily.

- Fresh vanilla pods are expensive, there is no getting around it, so be frugal and reuse the bean several times as it will still impart a lovely flavour. Simply wash the bean quickly under water and pat it dry, then put it into a jar of caster sugar and seal. The vanilla pod will keep beautifully and flavour the sugar to boot.

- A good vanilla pod should be plump, soft, pliable, shiny and have a heady vanilla aroma. At all costs avoid tiny, brittle vanilla pods.

Summer Trifle with Berries and Crunchy Meringues

This is a brilliantly easy dessert that appeals to the soul and makes the most of the best of summer's berries. It's my take on the great Aussie pav in the form of a trifle with berries and cream. Doesn't get any better than this!

1 Preheat a fan-forced oven to 130°C. Line a baking tray with baking paper.

2 For the meringues, whisk the egg whites and sugar in a stainless-steel bowl for 5–10 minutes with hand-held electric beaters until the mixture is silky and stiff peaks form. Transfer to a piping bag fitted with a 1 cm plain nozzle, then pipe small 1.5 cm wide × 1.5 cm high meringues out onto the baking paper. Bake for 45 minutes or until crisp on the outside and still soft in the centre. Makes about 30.

3 Bring half of the berries and the caster sugar to the boil in a small saucepan over medium heat. Simmer for 6 minutes or until the sugar dissolves and the berries collapse. Puree the berry mixture in a blender.

4 Whisk the mascarpone, cream and vanilla seeds with hand-held electric beaters until soft peaks form, then set aside. Crush the biscuits and drizzle with the Amaretto.

5 Spoon or pipe a little of the berry puree into the base of 4 glasses, then spoon in some of the cream mixture. Add some of the berries and a little more cream, then add a layer of biscuits. Repeat this layering process until all the cream mixture, berry puree, berries and biscuits are used. Pile a few meringues high on each trifle and serve.

Serves 4

250 g strawberries
150 g raspberries
150 g blackberries
150 g caster sugar
200 g mascarpone
200 ml pouring cream
1 vanilla pod, split and
    seeds scraped
10 amaretti biscuits
75 ml Amaretto

CRUNCHY MERINGUES
6 free-range egg whites
250 g caster sugar

Notes

- *I remember trifle was a standby for Mum when we had visitors over summer and it's a standby for me today because it is so versatile. Here you have a dessert that, as things come into season, can be transformed into something different each time you make it. In summer think mangoes, blackberries, cherries, peaches, raspberries and gooseberries, while in autumn think plums.*

- *A trifle can include just about anything sweet really – custard, jelly, fruit, cream, soft sponge or crunchy biscuits. Tiramisu is technically a trifle, although a few Italians may feel compromised by that fact!*

Chicken Stock

Makes 1.8 litres

1 kg free-range chicken bones,
    chopped into 5 cm pieces
2 litres water
1 stick celery, finely chopped
1 onion, finely chopped
½ bulb garlic
1 fresh bay leaf
2 sprigs thyme
8 white peppercorns

Notes

· *To boost the flavour, you can*
make what we call a double
chicken stock. Strain the first
stock, discarding the solids,
then repeat the process with
a fresh set of raw chicken
bones. The resulting stock
will make the best chicken
soup you have ever tasted!

The chicken stock I've given here is a white chicken stock as it is based on raw bones. It is probably the easiest stock to make and, because of its delicate and fairly neutral flavour, it is super-versatile in the home kitchen. It can be used for soups, sauces and, if not too strongly flavoured, it crosses nicely over to being used in seafood-based dishes that require fish stock, resulting in a lovely depth of flavour that is not overly fishy. Chicken stock does not require a long cooking time – it is all about preserving the fresh flavour of the chicken, vegetables and aromats.

1   Bring the chicken bones and water to the boil in a heavy-based stockpot over high heat. Skim any impurities from the surface and discard. Add the celery, onion, garlic, bay leaf, thyme and peppercorns. Gently simmer the stock over low heat for 2 hours, skimming the surface once or twice to remove the fat.

2   Turn off the heat and leave to cool for approximately 40 minutes. Strain the stock through a fine sieve, discarding the bones and vegetables, then leave to cool completely. Transfer the stock to airtight containers, then seal, label and date. Store in the fridge for up to 5 days or freezer for up to 2 months.

Fish Stock

Makes 1.8 litres

1 kg white fish bones (no heads),
    such as snapper, whiting or blue-
    eye trevalla, chopped along the
    spine into 4–5 sections
1 tablespoon olive oil
1 small leek, white part only,
    half lengthways, washed well,
    thinly sliced
1 small bulb fennel, trimmed,
    thinly sliced
1 small onion, thinly sliced
2 star anise
4–5 sprigs thyme
1 bay leaf
1 teaspoon sea salt flakes
1 teaspoon white peppercorns
100 ml dry white wine
2 litres water

I don't often make fish stock as most of my family find its flavour a little too fishy, so I tend to use a light chicken stock instead. However, fish stock does add a lovely depth of flavour to seafood-based dishes such as risotto, soups and, of course, fish sauces. If you are anything like my Mum, who hates the smell of fish permeating the house, then make this stock outside on the barbecue hotplate. This may sound strange, but you have been warned!

1   Wash the fish bones under cold running water for 1–2 minutes to remove any blood and impurities. Drain and set aside. Heat the olive oil in a stockpot over medium heat, then add the leek, fennel, onion, fish bones, star anise, thyme, bay leaf, salt and pepper. Cook for 3 minutes or until the spices release their aroma. Add the wine, then bring to the boil and pour in the water. Bring to the boil, skimming any impurities from the surface as it begins to boil. Reduce the heat to low and simmer for 20 minutes. Remove the stock from the heat and leave to stand for 5 minutes. Strain carefully into a large bowl through a fine strainer or muslin cloth, then cool quickly. Transfer the stock to airtight containers, then seal, label and date and store in the fridge for up to 4 days or freezer for up to 2 months.

Basic Pasta Dough

A pasta machine is essential for rolling dough as it can be difficult to achieve the correct texture by hand-rolling with a rolling pin unless you are very experienced. Secure the pasta machine firmly to your kitchen bench and make sure that it is calibrated so that the rollers are spaced evenly to ensure your pasta is of an even thickness. When passing and folding the dough through the machine, it becomes increasingly thinner and develops an even texture – this is called laminating. This is a crucial process that makes for a smooth and elastic dough.

Serves 4

200 g plain flour, plus extra for dusting
1 pinch table salt
2 × 55 g free-range eggs
2 teaspoons olive oil
2 teaspoons water

1   Blend the flour, salt and eggs in a food processor until combined. Add the oil and water and blend until the mixture has a fine and moist crumb-like consistency. Turn the dough out onto a lightly floured bench and knead into a ball – it should be cohesive, smooth and elastic. Press the dough down to flatten and form a rough rectangle. Wrap the dough in plastic film and leave to rest for 30 minutes.

2   Sprinkle a little flour on the bench and unwrap the dough. Use a rolling pin lightly dusted with flour, to roll and elongate the rectangle so that it will pass through the first setting of the pasta machine more easily.

3   Feed the dough through the rollers of a pasta machine set at the widest setting, turning the handle and teasing the rolled dough along the bench as it feeds through the machine.

4   Brush the flour off the pasta sheet, then fold one end over onto the centre and press it down. Fold the other end over the top and press it down, then feed the dough through the machine on the same setting. Repeat this process twice. Fold the dough and feed it through the rollers, reducing the setting each time, making the dough thinner, until you reach the second-last setting. If you find the dough length difficult to manage, then cut it into manageable lengths and work in batches, covering the pasta pieces with a tea towel.

5   The dough can be left in sheets if you wish to make lasagne or filled pasta (such as the tortellini on page 68), or cut into pappardelle, fettucine or tagliatelle, depending on what you are making – just follow the cutting instructions for your machine or cut by hand as required. Transfer the pasta to a lightly floured baking tray and repeat with the remaining 3 pieces of dough.

Basic Sweet Pastry

Makes enough to line
a 26–28 cm tart tin

125 g unsalted butter, softened
30 g icing sugar
240 g plain flour
pinch of table salt
1 free-range egg
250 g rice or baking beans,
    for blind baking

1 Place the butter in the bowl of an electric mixer fitted with a paddle attachment (or use a food processor). Add the icing sugar and mix until creamy, then add the flour and salt. Mix for 30 seconds and then add the egg, continuing to mix for 2 minutes or until the dough comes together to form a ball.

2 Either proceed with the recipe you are making from this book, or, if you wish to blind-bake the pastry case, tear off two 30 cm × 30 cm sheets baking paper. Roll the dough with a rolling pin between the baking paper sheets until 3 mm thick. To line a tart tin with the dough, peel off one sheet of the paper and turn the other sheet, dough-side down, over the tin, then gently ease the dough into the tin. Remove the remaining paper and mould the pastry up the sides of the tin with your fingertips, reserving the baking paper. Remove any excess pastry with your thumbs by pressing down along the edge of tin. Chill in the fridge for 30 minutes.

3 Preheat a fan-forced oven to 160°C.

4 Press the sheet of reserved baking paper onto the pastry, then fill with rice or baking beans and blind bake for 15 minutes or until golden. Remove from the oven, take out the baking beans and remove the paper, then leave the pastry case to cool. Proceed with the recipe.

Goat's Cheese Fondant

Makes about 180 ml

1 teaspoon olive oil
2 shallots, finely chopped
25 ml sherry vinegar
50 ml pouring cream
150 g soft goat's cheese,
    crumbled

I often make a herby version of this goat's cheese fondant that is reminiscent of a cheese they make in France called *cervelle de canu*. If you want to give this a go, add a generous handful of picked herbs such as dill, chervil, chives and tarragon and a teaspoon of freshly ground white pepper, then blend until the mixture is smooth and green. Either version is great spread onto grilled sourdough or served as a dip with crisp, peppery radishes or crackers. The fondant also makes a nice centrepiece to an entree in its own right, served with some frisee, crisp bacon, walnuts and a drizzle of Basic Vinaigrette (see page 180).

1 Heat the oil in a small frying pan over low heat, then cook the shallot for 2 minutes or until translucent, stirring occasionally. Add the vinegar and leave to reduce for 2 minutes, then add the cream and simmer for 2 minutes or until the mixture has reduced by half. Remove from the heat and cool. Blend the shallot mixture and goat's cheese in a blender or food processor until smooth and creamy. Cover with plastic film and chill in the fridge.

Grape, Ginger and Mustard Chutney

I love a nice chutney or relish. They are a good standby to add a bit of pizzazz to cold meat, cheese or a hot pie or sausage roll. Make 'em, keep 'em and enjoy!

1   Heat the vinegar, mustard seeds and sugar in a saucepan over medium heat, stirring until the sugar dissolves. Add the fennel, shallot, grapes and ginger to the pan. Bring the mixture to the boil and simmer gently for 45 minutes or until glossy and sweet. Remove from the heat and pour into a 500 ml-capacity sterilised container, then leave to cool. Unopened jars of this chutney can be stored in a cool, dark place for up to 4 months. Once opened, store in the fridge for up to 2 months.

Makes 500 ml

80 ml champagne vinegar
2 teaspoons mustard seeds
220 g soft brown sugar
½ bulb fennel, shredded
4 shallots, thinly sliced
200 g red or green grapes, halved and seeded (if necessary)
1 small knob ginger, peeled and shredded

Tomato Chutney

For the home cook, making your own chutneys and jams can be such a thrill. They seem complicated but are in fact quite easy to make. Not only are they a great standby to spice up the simplest of dishes, but they make great gifts and your friends will think you are very clever. If anybody can remember their granny making chutneys you may recall her pouring it into hot sterilised jars, then cooling it and popping on the lid. A well made chutney will last if stored like this, unopened and in a cool pantry, for months. Once opened, it is best to store this chutney in the fridge for up to three weeks, and use a clean spoon every time you serve it.

1   Cut a small cross on the base of the tomatoes, remove the core and place in a large bowl. Cover with boiling water and leave for 10 seconds. Drain and rinse with cold water, then peel. Chop the tomatoes into small pieces and discard the skin and seeds.

2   Warm the olive oil in a saucepan over a low heat. Add the onions, garlic and a pinch of salt, then cook for 3–4 minutes or until translucent. Stir in the tomato paste, then add the sugar, vinegar, star anise, cloves and cinnamon. Cook for a further 2 minutes to combine all the flavours. Add the tomato. Simmer for 50 minutes over low heat until the chutney is glossy and has a jam-like consistency.

3   Remove from the heat and leave to cool. Transfer to a small bowl and serve. Unopened jars of this chutney can be stored in a cool, dark place for up to 4 months. Once opened, store in the fridge for up to 3 weeks.

Makes 500 ml

7 ripe tomatoes
boiling water, to cover
50 ml olive oil
1 onion, finely diced
3 cloves garlic, finely sliced
table salt
2 tablespoons tomato paste
50 g soft brown sugar
50 ml white-wine vinegar
2 star anise
3 cloves
2 cinnamon sticks

Notes
· *The trick to making chutney is to find the right balance between the vinegar and sugar. Generally, the higher the concentration of sugar or vinegar, the longer the preserve will last.*

Kasundi Chutney

Makes 1.25 litres

1 clove
3 cardamom pods
2 teaspoons cumin seeds
250 ml olive oil
4 onions, roughly chopped
2 teaspoons mustard seeds
1 cinnamon stick
2 teaspoons chilli flakes
2 teaspoons turmeric
2 fresh long thin red chillies
knob of ginger, peeled and
    roughly chopped
2 cloves garlic, peeled
50 g soft brown sugar
50 ml white-wine vinegar
1 × 800 g tin chopped tomato
2 eggplants, chopped
table salt
½ cup coriander, roughly chopped

Note
• *If bottled in a sterilised jar,
  this spicy little number
  will keep unopened in
  a cool, dark pantry for
  up to 3 months.*

This is a spicy chutney but I have erred on the side of caution, so if you like, boost the fresh chilli and the mustard seeds to give it more of a kick. It works well with grilled chicken or fish, or can be served as a dip with warm Turkish or pita bread.

1 Dry-roast the clove, cardamom and cumin in a frying pan over high heat for 2 minutes or until aromatic, then crush with a mortar and pestle and set aside.

2 Put 100 ml of the olive oil in a large heavy-based saucepan, then add the onion, the clove, cardamom and cumin mixture, mustard seeds, cinnamon stick and chilli flakes and cook over medium heat for 2–3 minutes or until the onion softens. Add the turmeric and cook for a further 3–4 minutes, stirring occasionally.

3 Puree the chillies, ginger and garlic with 1 tablespoon of the olive oil in a food processor. Add the puree to the pan of frying spices and stir through. Add the sugar, vinegar and tomato. Stir to combine, then reduce the heat to low and cook for 30 minutes, stirring occasionally.

4 Meanwhile, place the eggplant in a colander and sprinkle with salt, then leave for 30 minutes. Rinse the eggplant and pat dry with paper towel.

5 Heat the remaining olive oil in a large non-stick frying pan over high heat and fry the eggplant for 20 minutes or until golden. Drain the eggplant on paper towel and add to the chutney. Cook for a further 10 minutes until thickened. Add the coriander and remove from the heat, then leave to cool.

6 Transfer the kasundi to a sterilised 1.25 litre-capacity jar, then store in the fridge for up to 3 weeks; use a clean spoon every time you serve it.

Home-style Mash

This is how I make my mash at home when I'm trying to be good – when I'm in the restaurant I add lashings of butter as this improves the flavour no end but, sadly, this is no good for the waistline.

The number one rule for perfect mash is to use new-season potatoes (see page 196) because they result in the softest, fluffiest texture. As potatoes get older their texture changes and sugar content increases. As a result, they can become gluey when mashed and their flavour is not the best.

1   Place the potato in a saucepan and cover with cold water. Add the salt and bring to the boil over high heat. Reduce the heat to low and simmer for 20 minutes or until tender. Strain the potato in a colander, reserving a little of the water. Return the potato to the pan, then pop the lid on and keep warm.

2   Meanwhile, bring the milk and olive oil to the boil and turn off the heat. Keep warm.

3   Mash the warm potato with a masher or press it through a fine sieve or potato ricer over a bowl. Add the hot milk mixture and butter to the pan and use a whisk to whip the potato until smooth. Add a little of the reserved potato water if the mixture is stiff. Whisk until smooth and fluffy. Serve.

Serves 4

2 large desire potatoes,
    cut into quarters
1 teaspoon table salt
80 ml milk
2 tablespoons extra virgin olive oil
40 g unsalted butter

Notes

- *Mashing potato while it is still hot releases the steam and bursts the starches, making for a light and fluffy mash. Changes in temperature affect the starch in spuds and they can go lumpy or gluey, so work quickly and serve at once.*

Pangrattato

Pangrattato can be labelled 'poor man's parmesan'. Traditionally in the South of Italy, where they don't use a whole lot of cheese in their cooking, pangrattato is quite common. Essentially, this crisp, flavoured toasted breadcrumb mixture not only uses up stale bread, but it adds a delicious crunchy topping for a number of savoury dishes, adding both texture and flavour. The addition of lemon, garlic and salts also adds another dimension to the flavour.

1   Preheat a fan-forced oven 180°C.

2   Place the bread in a heavy-based roasting pan, then drizzle with olive oil. Add the thyme leaves, a good pinch of salt and a few turns of pepper. Toast in the oven for 15 minutes or until golden and crisp, stirring once or twice to ensure the pieces colour evenly. Transfer to paper towel to drain. Set aside.

Serves 4

200 g dense sourdough bread,
    torn into small pieces
60 ml olive oil
2 sprigs thyme, leaves picked
sea salt flakes and freshly ground
    white pepper

Vanilla Ice Cream

Makes 1 litre

crushed ice
500 ml pouring cream
500 ml milk
75 g glucose (see page 196)
1 vanilla pod, split
12 free-range egg yolks
100 g caster sugar

Notes

- *Because ice cream is often based on custard made with fresh eggs it is important to heat the custard to at least 80°C, then to cool it as quickly as possible, which is why I cool it over ice. This knocks the temperature down quickly and prevents the custard from scrambling, and prevents the growth of harmful bacteria. As soon as the custard is cold it should be refrigerated or frozen immediately in your ice cream machine.*

- *I pour half of the cream and milk into the egg yolks, then whisk them together before transferring the lot to the pan of hot cream and milk because this helps to maintain the temperature in the pan, which means that it doesn't take a long time for the custard to thicken. If you pour all of the hot cream and milk into the egg yolks, by the time you whisk the mixture and return it to the pan, the temperature will have dropped considerably, meaning the custard will take longer to thicken.*

The key to making great ice cream is starting with a good custard. A candy thermometer is a worthwhile investment when making custards because reaching the right temperature guarantees that the custard is sterilised and the eggs will thicken. One of the most common mistakes when making custard is not cooling it quickly enough, thus resulting in something resembling scrambled eggs. You will also need to have an ice cream machine in your gadget cupboard for this one.

1 Have two bowls ready, one a little larger than the other. Place the crushed ice into the larger bowl and have a fine mesh sieve next to the stove. Bring the cream, milk, glucose and vanilla pod to the boil in a heavy-based saucepan over high heat.

2 Meanwhile, in the smaller bowl, whisk the egg yolks and sugar until pale and fluffy. Quickly pour half of the hot cream mixture into the egg mixture and whisk to combine, then quickly pour the egg mixture back into the pan with the remaining hot cream mixture.

3 Place the empty bowl over the ice. Turn the heat to low and whisk the cream mixture until it registers 82°C on a candy thermometer; this takes approximately 2 minutes. If you do not have a candy thermometer, stir the mixture with a wooden spoon then, as the custard heats and thickens, wipe the back of the spoon with your finger; there should be a clear track that does not close up. Pour the custard immediately through the sieve into the bowl sitting over the ice. Whisk the custard 2–3 times to knock out some heat quickly. Leave it to cool over the ice until completely cold, stirring occasionally.

4 Pour the cold custard into an ice cream machine and churn according to the manufacturer's instructions.

Lemon Mascarpone Ice Cream

Combining the rich creaminess of mascarpone and tanginess of lemon zest, this is one of my all-time favourite ice cream flavours. I like to serve it alongside the Crepes with Passionfruit Syrup on page 170 or just eat large scoops of it on its own.

Makes 1 litre

crushed ice
300 ml milk
300 ml pouring cream
300 g condensed milk
1 vanilla pod, split
8 free-range egg yolks
150 g caster sugar
300 g mascarpone
finely grated zest of 3 lemons

1   Have two bowls ready, one a little larger than the other. Place the crushed ice into the larger bowl and have a fine mesh sieve next to the stove. Bring the cream, milk, condensed milk and vanilla pod to the boil in a heavy-based saucepan over high heat.

2   Meanwhile, in the smaller bowl, whisk the egg yolks and sugar until pale and fluffy. Quickly pour half of the hot cream mixture into the egg mixture and whisk to combine, then quickly pour the egg mixture back into the pan with the remaining hot cream mixture.

3   Place the empty bowl over the ice. Turn the heat to low and whisk the cream mixture until it registers 82°C on a candy thermometer; this takes approximately 2 minutes. If you do not have a candy thermometer, stir the mixture with a wooden spoon then, as the custard heats and thickens, wipe the back of the spoon with your finger; there should be a clear track that does not close up. Pour the custard immediately through a fine strainer into the bowl sitting over the ice. Whisk the custard 2–3 times to knock out some of the heat quickly. Leave it to cool over the ice until completely cold, stirring occasionally.

4   Add the mascarpone and lemon zest to the custard. Whisk until smooth.

5   Pour the cold custard into an ice cream machine and churn according to the manufacturer's instructions.

Notes

- *Because ice cream is often based on custard made with fresh eggs it is important to heat the custard to at least 80°C, then to cool it as quickly as possible, which is why I cool it over ice. This knocks the temperature down quickly and prevents the custard from scrambling, and prevents the growth of harmful bacteria. As soon as the custard is cold it should be refrigerated or frozen immediately in your ice cream machine.*

Caramel Ice Cream

Makes 1 litre

300 g sugar
crushed ice
500 ml pouring cream
500 ml milk
10 free-range egg yolks
75 g caster sugar

Notes

• *Because ice cream is often based on custard made with fresh eggs it is important to heat the custard to at least 80°C, then to cool it as quickly as possible, which is why I cool it over ice. This knocks the temperature down quickly and prevents the custard from scrambling, and prevents the growth of harmful bacteria. As soon as the custard is cold it should be refrigerated or frozen immediately in your ice cream machine.*

Use this luscious caramel ice cream to make the Espresso and Caramel Ice Cream Sandwiches on page 168 – it will taste so much better if you've made the ice cream yourself.

1 Fill the sink or a bowl large enough to fit the saucepan you are using to make the caramel with 2 cm cold water.

2 Sprinkle the sugar evenly over the base of a large heavy-based saucepan. Melt the sugar over high heat until a light-amber tinge forms, then stir the sugar until it turns a dark-caramel colour – you are looking for a dark, reddish-brown colour. Immediately immerse the base of the pan into the cold water and leave for 1 minute to cool. Remove the pan from the water, then set aside.

3 Have 2 bowls ready, 1 a little larger than the other. Place the crushed ice into the larger bowl and have a fine mesh sieve next to the stove.

4 Add the cream and milk to the pan of caramel, then bring to the boil over medium heat and stir until the caramel has dissolved.

5 In the smaller bowl, whisk the egg yolks and caster sugar until pale and fluffy. Quickly pour half of the hot cream mixture into the egg mixture and whisk to combine, then quickly pour the egg mixture back into the pan with the remaining hot cream mixture.

6 Place the empty bowl over the ice. Turn the heat to low and whisk the cream mixture until it registers 82°C on a candy thermometer; this takes approximately 2 minutes. If you do not have a candy thermometer, stir the mixture with a wooden spoon then, as the custard heats and thickens, wipe the back of the spoon with your finger; there should be a clear track that does not close up. Pour the custard immediately through a fine strainer into the bowl sitting over the ice. Whisk the custard 2–3 times to knock out some of the heat quickly. Leave it to cool over the ice until completely cold, stirring occasionally.

7 Pour the cold custard into an ice cream machine and churn according to the manufacturer's instructions.

Glossary

Beans – cooking dried

When cooking dried beans and pulses I follow a couple of simple rules: rinse the beans well but avoid soaking all but the hardiest of dried beans, such as borlotti beans, kidney beans and lima beans. Softer pulses such as lentils, split peas and small white beans do not need to be soaked. Soaking also cleans the beans as they can be quite dirty, so remember to rinse after soaking. Some cooks advocate adding bicarbonate of soda to the soaking water as they say it aids digestion and speeds up the cooking process. I don't think this necessary as beans such as cannellini beans lose their skins. To cook, transfer the drained beans to a large saucepan, then cover with cold water. Bring to the boil, then simmer for 45 minutes or until tender. Drain. Don't add salt during cooking as this toughens the beans. Season them at the end of cooking instead.

Belachan

Otherwise known as shrimp paste, this stinky, salty paste is made from fermented dried prawns or krill pressed into blocks. Widely used across South-East Asia, from Indonesia, Thailand and Malaysia through to Vietnam and southern China, it adds saltiness and complexity to dishes. It is generally roasted, grilled or fried before it is added to a dish. Available from Asian food stores and larger supermarkets.

Broken rice

Broken rice is a common ingredient in Vietnamese cooking. Because the rice is literally broken it cooks very quickly. It absorbs the same amount of water during cooking as long-grain rice, that is, a ratio of two parts water to one part rice. I love the couscous-like texture of broken rice and use it often when I cook at home. Available from Asian food stores.

Chinese sausage (*lap cheung*)

A sweet, red, dried pork sausage. There are a several different varieties but the most commonly available are Cantonese. They are quite hard and tight but develop a lovely flavour when sliced, steamed, grilled or fried on their own or as part of more complex dishes. Available from Asian food stores and larger supermarkets.

Chocolate – couverture

The best chocolate that you can buy is a couverture because, by its very nature, it is determined by law that it must contain a minimum of thirty-two per cent cocoa butter and fifty-four per cent combined total of cocoa solids and cocoa butter. The more cocoa butter and solids means less sugar and ultimately more flavour. Like a fine wine, a good couverture will melt and disappear away from your tongue, leaving a heady, deep chocolate flavour. Cooking chocolate on the other hand contains a lot more sugar, vegetable oils and possibly artificial flavourings. Like most foods it's all horses for courses – it's neither right nor wrong to enjoy one above the other and, of course, price will play an important part in the choice. We use both widely at the restaurants.

Index

LANTERN

Published by the Penguin Group
Penguin Group (Australia)
250 Camberwell Road, Camberwell, Victoria 3124, Australia
(a division of Pearson Australia Group Pty Ltd)
Penguin Group (USA) Inc.
375 Hudson Street, New York, New York 10014, USA
Penguin Group (Canada)
10 Alcorn Avenue, Toronto, Ontario, Canada M4V 3B2
(a division of Pearson Penguin Canada Inc.)
Penguin Books Ltd
80 Strand, London WC2R 0RL, England
Penguin Ireland
25 St Stephen's Green, Dublin 2, Ireland
(a division of Penguin Books Ltd)
Penguin Books India Pvt Ltd
11 Community Centre, Panchsheel Park, New Delhi – 110 017, India
Penguin Group (NZ)
Cnr Airborne and Rosedale Roads, Albany, Auckland, New Zealand
(a division of Pearson New Zealand Ltd)
Penguin Books (South Africa) (Pty) Ltd
24 Sturdee Avenue, Rosebank, Johannesburg 2196, South Africa

Penguin Books Ltd, Registered Offices: 80 Strand, London WC2R 0RL, England

First published by Penguin Group (Australia), a division of Pearson Australia Group Pty Ltd, 2010

1 3 5 7 9 10 8 6 4 2

Copyright © Gary Mehigan 2010
Photography copyright © Dean Cambray 2010
Front cover photography and photography on pages ii, iv, x, xiii, xiv, xv, xvi,
40, 58, 78, 112, 134, 178, 192, 193, 200, 201 copyright © Adrian Lander 2010
Photography on pages vi–vii courtesy of Gary Mehigan

Design by John Canty © Penguin Group (Australia)
Design coordination by Evi O.
Styling by Fiona Hammond
Front cover styling by Jane Hann
Typeset in Adobe Caslon Pro and Adobe Garamond
by Post Pre-press Group, Brisbane, Queensland
Printed in China by the South China Printing Company

National Library of Australia
Cataloguing-in-Publication data:

Mehigan, Gary, 1967 –
Gary Mehigan's Comfort Food.
1st ed.
ISBN 9781921382321 (hbk.)
Includes index.
Comfort food, Cookery.

641.5

penguin.com.au/lantern